The Making of a Good Man

Lessons in Life and Integrity

Roy S. Rogers

https://striveipg.com/

Copyright © 2024 Roy S. Rogers

Author's website: https://bookemdoubler.com/
Author's email: DBLR.ROGERS@GMAIL.COM

All Rights Reserved. No part of this publication may be reproduced, distributed, or transmitted in any form or by any means, including photocopying, recording, or other electronic or mechanical methods, without the prior written permission of the publisher, except in the case of brief quotations embodied in critical reviews and certain other noncommercial uses permitted by copyright law.

Strive Publishing is a division of Courageous Media Group. For more information on the authors, ordering, book signings, or to sponsor an event, email info@courageouswomanmag.com.

ISBN: 979-8-218-52001-4

Edited by Shonell Bacon and Nelecia Murrell, Ed.D.
Formatted by Shonell Bacon

Publisher/Book Coach – Telishia Berry; you can contact Telishia for more publishing information via her website,
www.courageouswomanmag.com.

Dedication

To my village.

Acknowledgments

First and foremost, I thank God for guiding me to make a meaningful and lasting impact on the lives of young men.

My heartfelt gratitude goes to my wife for standing by my side as I tirelessly worked on this endeavor. Deep appreciation for my parents for providing me with a sound, nurturing foundation. Immense thanks to my grandparents for being steadfast family heads who led by example. Your influence has shaped who I am today.

Dr. Nelecia Murrell, your encouragement and belief in me pushed me to achieve greater heights. Your support throughout this journey was truly inspirational.

To the Kappa Alpha Psi fraternity and my line, La Renaissance 11, thank you for always holding me accountable and being examples of great men.

My family, you are the reason I stand firm in my purpose today. To my friends, you inspire and spur me on toward good deeds.

I am deeply grateful to everyone who has supported me along the way. My life is enriched because of your contributions.

Foreword

In reflecting on the blessings that have shaped my life, I find myself in awe of the divine guidance that has led me through both triumphs and trials. From the thrill of playing in the National Football League to the profound responsibility of serving as a magistrate judge in a politically and racially charged environment, I recognize a recurring truth: these experiences were not mere coincidences but the manifestation of God's plan. I have always believed that when we follow our heart and heed God's voice, our path unfolds in remarkable ways.

It was in this spirit of divine orchestration that I met Rogers in 2008. I dubbed him "Denzel" for his charismatic presence and soulful cadence, reminiscent of the actor Denzel Washington. Rogers, as my police academy instructor, embodied a dedication to exploring life's new chapters that has been nothing short of inspiring. I eagerly anticipate witnessing how God continues to elevate him, as he inspires countless others to follow in his footsteps.

Rogers's book, The Making of a Good Man: Lessons in Life and Integrity moved me deeply. Though my upbringing was different, the heartfelt essence of this book resonates with my own experiences as a father. Rogers's portrayal of a loving father-son relationship struck a chord with me, drawing parallels to the way I strive to embrace and guide my own children.

In The Making of a Good Man: Lessons in Life and Integrity, Rogers masterfully captures the profound beauty of a father-son bond. For those who may have missed out on a paternal relationship, his vivid storytelling offers a window into what such a connection can be. The book is a testament to the wisdom passed down through generations, highlighting the essential role of nurturing grandparents, parents, and a supportive community in shaping a child's future. Rogers's narrative embodies the truth that "it takes a village to raise a child," making it a must-read that will bring both joy and reflection to its readers.

Michael L. Scurlock

Contents

The Question	1
Phase One	**11**
Reflections of Life's Lessons	12
The Ring and the Paddle	16
Bonds Woven in the Tapestry of Youth	20
Echoes of a Patriarch's Legacy	23
Tapestry Woven with Generations of Love	27
Summer Tale of Camp, Crushes, and Catches	31
The Mouse, the Bond, and the Promise	34
The Art of Protection	38
A Legacy of Love: From Fishing Tales to Love Stories	45
A Sunday Serenade of Stories	50
Phase Two	**54**
Sunday Table Talks	55
Trails of Reflection	59
A First Crush Memory	62
Lessons Learned on the Block	64
Lessons in Responsibility and Financial Wisdom	68
Entrepreneurship and Financial Discipline	73
Elderly Treasures	77
Trash Turned Treasure	82
Sporting Tales and Community Bonds	86
Academic Excellence and Teamwork	93
Triumph on the Track	99
A Runner's Escape	106

A Gift on Four Wheels	109
Marching to a Different Beat	112
Navigating through Adversity to Manhood	115
Beecher High: A Blast from the Past	119
Summer Days and College Dreams	123
Phase Three	**128**
Journey to Adulthood: From Beecher to College	129
Lessons Learned by the Lake: From Fishing to Freshman Year	133
Crossing the Burning Sands: A Journey into Greek Life	139
Brotherhood beyond Bloodlines	150
College Adventures: Stepping Up to Challenges	154
College and Life Decisions	159
The Value of Integrity	162
Fireside Feasts and Family Bonds	164
Rite of Passage and Life Targets	169
Passing the Torch	176
The Art of Instruction	179
Forging the Elite: Sonny's Cadre Legacy	182
Carrying the Torch: A Lifetime of Service and Sacrifice	190

The Question

The evening in the cozy family home was like many others. Roy, a curious eight-year-old, had just devoured his dinner and was now playing with his beloved pet hamster, Gobbles. Roy's great grandma, Granny, a wise and gentle presence in the household, had retreated to her room for her nightly dose of soothing jazz before calling it a night. Meanwhile, Roy's mom, Marsha, was busy in the kitchen, engaged in her nightly call with her best friend, Sandra.

However, the night would be different for Roy.

Toward the tail end of Marsha's call, she relished with distinct conviction, "I know. He truly is a good man."

This wasn't the first time Roy had heard her say these words, but tonight, he was determined to ask her to explain.

With piqued curiosity and firm resolve, Roy asked, "Momma, how can I become a good man?" He adored his mom and wanted to make her proud. Although he was just a boy, he felt a deep desire to learn what it took to become a good man.

Slightly taken aback by Roy's question, Marsha recognized that her son was genuinely seeking answers. She replied, "Son, that's an excellent question. I could try to explain, but I think I know someone who can do a better job because she helped many young boys like you grow up to be great men."

With those words, Marsha took Roy into Granny's room, where the soft notes of jazz filled the air. She encouraged him to repeat his question.

Beaming with pride, Granny gently settled Roy on her lap, and began, "That's a big question for a little boy like you, but I think I might have some answers. Many moons ago, I knew a little boy named Sonny. When he was about your age, people would say he had the strength and courage of a lion."

Roy, eager for the story, interjected, "Really ... why?"

Granny continued with a smile, "I'm going to tell you about some of the things he did, and I want you to tell me if you, too, feel he was strong and courageous."

After an eager nod from Roy, Granny narrated, "His Uncle Tracey called him Running Fox, but everyone else called him Sonny." She then painted a vivid picture of Sonny's early life, where he showed kindness by helping neighbors, adding, "Sonny spent most of his early childhood with his grandparents because his dad was a soldier fighting in the Vietnam War, and his mom worked long hours. But his dad called frequently so that Sonny would know his voice."

Curious, Roy asked, "What was Sonny like in school?"

Granny continued with a twinkle in her eye, "When Sonny started school, all the families would watch the children get on the bus. He had to speak to everyone before he got on the bus. He was very polite and friendly. I still remember his first day of school. The teacher said she asked all the children their names and where they lived. When it was Sonny's turn to share, he said, 'I don't know, and I don't care.' Judging from Sonny's dismissive response, his teacher thought school was going to be a challenge for little Sonny."

Granny paused, and Roy leaned forward, engrossed in the story. She continued, "But a very interesting thing happened as he got more comfortable. The teacher asked Sonny, 'What do you want to be when you grow up?' Sonny stood on his chair and in a loud voice proclaimed, 'I'm gonna be a police officer!' Listening to the teacher tell me about Sonny confirmed what I knew about him. Though he was extremely playful and light-spirited, he was also a very determined kid. He spoke with the conviction of someone who knew what he wanted. I honestly don't think I knew it then, but I believe he helped me realize a powerful truth."

Roy, puzzled by this revelation, asked, "How could a kid teach you a powerful truth, Granny?"

Granny smiled warmly at Roy's curiosity. "He showed me that the words I confess with my mouth can become a reality."

They both paused to reflect on the power of words. Roy broke the silence, asking, "So, did Sonny become a police officer, Granny?"

With an affectionate glance, Granny replied, "Do you want me to tell you now, or would you like to wait and see what happens?" Roy's curiosity was at its peak, but he decided to wait for Granny to continue with Sonny's story.

Granny then delved into Sonny's daily routine, describing how he would energetically run all the way home from the bus stop while other children walked. Remembering what

Granny shared earlier, Roy interjected, "So, is this why his uncle called him Running Fox?"

Granny chuckled. "You know what, Roy? I never thought to ask, but you might be right. It certainly makes sense."

Granny shared how his grandparents instilled in Sonny the value of hard work with daily chores and how he and his friends played football and wrestled in the neighborhood field. She fondly remembered the older boys, PJ, Rodney, Joe Joe, Shawn, and Juan, who played a significant role in Sonny's life, forming bonds like family.

"All of these young boys grew up to be good men," she said with gratification. "Those boys were so close; they even went to church together. The church was about seven blocks away from our block. As Sonny and PJ grew up, they walked to church together on Sundays. Sonny followed PJ because he was older and looked up to him.

"But PJ's grandparents made him go to church because they believed it was one of the ways we get closer to God. But contrary to PJ's grandparents' teachings, PJ and Sonny were mostly excited about walking to church to see all the little girls."

Despite their youthful motives, Granny explained how God's teachings found a way to reach them. "They were able to learn about His teachings, the ways He said they should behave and why. Church is a good place for young boys who want to grow up to be good men."

Granny vividly recalled how Sonny would recite Psalm 23 with unwavering conviction, breaking down each verse with profound insight. As she shared Sonny's interpretation with Roy, the depth of his understanding became evident.

"'The Lord is my shepherd,' Sonny would proclaim, affirming God's leadership in his life."

"'I shall not want,' signifying his trust in God's provision for all his needs."

"'He maketh me lie down in green pastures,' reflected Sonny's comfort in God's presence, providing peace amidst life's challenges."

"'He restoreth my soul,' symbolized Sonny's daily renewal, finding resilience and purpose in God's guidance."

Though Roy knew Psalm 23, he had never really considered how each line applied to his life the way Sonny interpreted it. Captivated by Granny's narrative, he couldn't help but wonder about the origin of Sonny's profound connection to Psalm 23. With curiosity burning in his eyes, he turned to Granny and asked if Sonny had learned it from someone at church.

Granny nodded in confirmation, explaining how Sonny's church leaders played a significant role in laying the foundation of his faith. Their teachings, combined with Sonny's innate curiosity and conviction, shaped his understanding of God's word and solidified his relationship with his Heavenly Father.

Roy, leaning in, captivated by the tales of this apparent flawless young boy, questioned, "Sonny seems to be the perfect kid, but surely he had a mischievous side, right?"

Granny nodded knowingly, her expression fond yet slightly admonishing. "Oh, he did indeed," she confirmed. "I remember one incident vividly."

She proceeded to recount the tale of Sonny's misadventure with the sink, while practicing his intent to outdo his friends in a peeing distance contest. "He was just being a boy," Granny explained, her tone understanding yet firm. "But he learned a valuable lesson that day."

Roy listened intently as Granny described Sonny's remorse and determination to make amends. "He realized the importance of taking responsibility for his actions," she concluded, her eyes meeting Roy's with a gentle wisdom. "And that's a lesson that stayed with him throughout his life."

While Roy was extremely intrigued by Granny's recap of Sonny's childhood, he was still laser focused on his initial question: what does it take to become a good man? Based on what Granny had shared so far, he had five takeaways:

- Be kind to those around you.
- When you know what you want to do with your life, proclaim it.
- Find friends who can double as family.
- Trust God and take Him at His word.
- Take responsibility for your actions.

However, in all of Granny's sharing, Roy couldn't help but wonder, who was Granny to Sonny? How did she know him so well? She said he spent most of his childhood with his grandparents because his parents could not be there—did that mean she was his caretaker? Or could it be that he was the grandson of one of the elderly people in the neighborhood? But just as he was about to ask Granny about how she knew Sonny, his mom returned to the room and announced, "Roy, your dad's home."

Granny and Roy had become so engrossed in Sonny's childhood stories that an hour had passed without their notice.

Roy eagerly ran to the door to greet his father, excited to share the stories Granny had been telling him about the boy named Sonny.

Granny joined them in the kitchen, where Roy enthusiastically recapped the tales she had shared. Roy's dad, Roy Sr., interjected with curiosity, addressing his grandmother, "Granny, who is this Sonny you've been telling my son about?"

Marsha, Roy Sr., and Granny exchanged telling smiles, hinting at a shared secret.

Roy suddenly had a realization and exclaimed, "Wait a second, is Sonny you, Dad? But your name is Roy, like mine."

With warmth and affirmation, Roy Sr. replied, "Yes, son, I'm the Sonny your Granny's been telling you about. When I was a kid, and even now, some of your aunts, uncles, and my friends call me Sonny."

That night, as Sonny tucked Roy into bed, Roy made his dad promise to tell him more stories about his childhood and how he grew up to be a good man. Sonny eagerly agreed, realizing that this was a precious opportunity to share valuable life lessons with his son.

As Sonny laid in bed that night, he contemplated the characteristics of a good man that he wanted to impart to his son: tenacity, mindfulness, vulnerability, emotional intelligence, trustworthiness, and above all, unwavering love. He knew that these qualities defined a good man, and he was determined to guide and mentor his son on the path to becoming one. With a sense of gratitude for this opportunity, he eagerly anticipated spending the weekend with Roy, sharing stories of his life and the experiences that had shaped him into the man his son admired and aspired to become.

Sonny knew the task of encapsulating how he embodies the characteristics of a good man was going to be challenging because in all honesty, he didn't always get it right. But he was determined to appease his son's curiosity and shed some light on what he'd learn throughout his life because all of his experiences (good, bad, and indifferent) worked together to make him the man he is. With that in mind, he drifted off to sleep, eager to spend the weekend with his son, recapping pivotal events in his life that empowered him to be a man his son was proud to call Dad.

PHASE ONE

Reflections of Life's Lessons

The sun's first rays danced upon the tranquil lake, casting a golden hue over the water as Roy and his father readied themselves for a memorable fishing trip. A father-son bonding opportunity awaited amidst the pristine serenity of the morning that promised a canvas for the stories and lessons Sonny held close to his heart.

As they cast their lines into the still waters, the gentle ripples mirrored the tales Sonny was about to share.

The air was filled with anticipation as Sonny began, his voice carrying the weight of experience. "Son, let me take you back to the beginning, to Pierson Elementary School. It was there my journey toward becoming a good man truly started."

Roy listened intently as his dad unraveled the layers of his early years.

"Granny noticed my curiosity early on and taught me to read even before school. I was a curious three-year-old, constantly asking 'Why?'

And like most kids, I wouldn't let go until I understood. Pierson Elementary became the place where my love for learning flourished."

As the fishing boat gently swayed, Sonny spoke fondly of Mr. Smith, the math teacher who became a beacon of inspiration. "'Learn it now, or it won't add up later,' Mr. Smith would say." Sonny chuckled. "I counted loose change twice to make sure I got it right. That mentality became one of my guiding principles."

Pausing, Sonny's eyes glimmered with nostalgia. "But it wasn't just about excelling; it was about doing your best in everything. I learned that lesson the hard way when I got a 'D' on an art project. I didn't take it seriously then, but later in life, I realized the importance of taking advantage of every opportunity I had to learn."

Sonny's stories wove through the fabric of Pierson Elementary, painting a picture of holistic growth. "It wasn't just about academics; it was also where I learned to swim, play sports, and face my fears head-on."

Roy's curiosity deepened, "What fears, Dad?"

Sonny shared the memory of his first swimming lesson. "Mr. Hamilton had all of us boys line up at the edge of the pool, the deep end. He then asked us to jump in one at a time; he was in the pool treading water. I jumped in, doggie-paddled to the side, and gradually built my confidence. It was a lesson in facing fear head-on, and with every awkward flail, Mr. Hamilton watchfully encouraged us to get to the wall of the pool."

Remembering another crucial challenge that helped shape his character during his elementary years, Sonny continued, "In the third grade, a boy spat in my face, and I punched him. Granny taught me a hard lesson that day about responding to cruelty with kindness."

Roy couldn't hide his disbelief. "But Dad, you were just defending yourself!"

Sonny nodded. "It might seem that way, but Granny taught me that kindness is a better response. Violence is never the answer."

As the fishing boat rocked gently on the water, Roy absorbed the lessons his father shared, realizing the depth of wisdom within each story. "So, it's about choosing how you respond, not letting the situation control your actions," Roy reflected.

Sonny beamed with pride at his son's understanding. "Exactly, son. It took me some time to grasp that lesson fully, but it made sense later, especially when I joined Martial Arts.

Martial Arts taught me how to defend myself, and oftentimes, this form of defense is intended to disarm one's opponents, not hurt them."

And so, father and son continued to cast their lines into the rippling lake, each story creating ripples of its own, weaving a tapestry of lessons, resilience, and the enduring bond between them.

The Ring and the Paddle

The morning sun cast a warm glow as Roy and his father sat on the lake, their fishing lines bobbing gently in the water. Sonny continued unraveling the tales of his elementary school days, a time when discipline and life lessons were dealt with in ways that might seem foreign to Roy.

"In our school," Sonny began, "Mr. Span was more than just a principal. He was a strong role model who taught us toughness and respect simultaneously. When we misbehaved, we got paddled."

Roy, wide-eyed, interrupted, "Your principal could hit you? And you let him?"

Sonny chuckled. "It was different back then, Roy. Paddling was a form of discipline for misbehavior. If we cut lines, were mean, or used curse words, we got paddled. It taught us that poor decisions had harsh consequences."

"I'm glad that's no longer a thing," Roy remarked, shaking his head.

Then Sonny's narrative shifted to the imposing figure of Mr. Wade, the physical education teacher. "He didn't accept 'I can't do it' excuses. One day, we had to climb a rope from the floor to the ceiling. It taught me the power of self-belief."

Recess, a time for physical play, introduced another character: Marvin, aka Too Short, the recess bully. Roy listened as his dad recounted a lunchtime challenge, a boxing match orchestrated by Principal Span himself.

"So, your principal organized boxing matches?!" Roy exclaimed, struggling to comprehend.

"Times were different, son. It wasn't about promoting violence but facing fears under supervision. It taught me to stand up to bullies in a controlled setting. This was an attempt at turning our apparent rivalry into a comradery."

Roy, skeptical, questioned if his dad became friends with Too Short after the match.

"Not exactly," Sonny admitted, "but facing him in that controlled setting forced me to confront my fears."

Roy couldn't help but compare his dad's elementary days to his. Minus the paddling, he could see a likeness in both of their experiences. However, of all the stories his dad had shared to this point, Roy still couldn't make peace with the fact that he was punished for defending himself when a kid spat on him. Roy thought of all the times he felt justified in defending himself, and this would definitely be one of those times.

So, he asked, "So, Dad, are you telling me there's never a good reason to fight?"

Realizing the weight of this question, Sonny reminded Roy of how Granny encouraged him to be kind. Adding, "I didn't know it then, but thinking back, and even as I grew into adulthood, I was never one to start a fight.

"Oddly enough, Principal Span may have been the first one to teach me how to use controlled fighting techniques to solve my differences."

But Roy challenged his dad's use of martial arts as a form of defense, saying "But, Dad, isn't martial arts also a form of fighting?"

Sonny nodded. "The difference between the two is the motive behind the fight: one is intended to physically hurt the person who did you wrong, while the other is intended to keep the other person from harming you."

Roy, still intrigued, questioned his dad about the supervised boxing matches, finding them bizarre in the context of his own school experiences.

"Were you made to fight, Dad?" Roy inquired. Sonny chuckled. "No, Son. It was about facing fears, not forcing fights. The takeaway was about character and courage."

As the fishing boat gently rocked on the lake, Roy and Sonny continued their conversation, weaving the threads of the past into a rich narrative of discipline, resilience, and the evolving nature of education. The lessons from Pierson Elementary, though unconventional by today's standards, had left an indelible mark on Sonny, shaping him into the man he had become.

Bonds Woven in the Tapestry of Youth

The morning mist lifted, revealing the shimmering dance of the sun on the tranquil lake. Roy and his dad sat patiently, their fishing lines idly drifting in the water. The lack of bites didn't dampen their spirits, for these fishing trips were less about the catch and more about the shared moments.

Roy, maintaining his curiosity about his dad's childhood, asked a question that unraveled details about Sonny's introduction to fishing.

"Dad, did you go fishing with your dad?"

Sonny, gazing at the glimmering lake, began weaving the tales of his summers spent with his mother. "Interestingly enough, my dad spent most of my childhood in Vietnam. I fished with my mom weekly, enduring the scorching heat and adverse conditions. These fishing trips with her taught me patience and focus."

As the fishing tales unfolded, Sonny recounted an unconventional pet, a turtle. His eyes sparkled with nostalgia as he recalled catching it with a fishhook, a misstep that led to a unique bond. "I realized a fishhook wasn't the best way to catch a turtle, but it was resilient. I made a space for it in the backyard like its fishing area. It taught me responsibility."

Much like Granny's lessons on hard work, Sonny spoke of the diligence required for fishing. "I had to dig worms, make worm beds, and be prepared. This taught me responsibility and readiness."

The narrative transitioned to Sonny's summer breaks spent with cousins, turning every activity into a spirited competition. "We played hard, raced in the streets, and challenged each other. Granny raised us like siblings. Family meant everything."

Sonny's eyes lit up as he spoke of the unbreakable bonds formed through shared competitions, discoveries, and adventures. "Our childhood bonds matured into a real unity. This is where I learned the value of family, that it takes a strong, loving village."

In addition to family, Sonny shared his experiences with the Big Brothers program, where Reverend Leo became a guiding figure.

The Making of a Good Man

"Reverend Leo was like an extension of my family, a positive role model. He introduced me to new experiences, including the Boy Scouts."

Sonny's voice resonated with gratitude as he delved into the impact of the Boy Scouts on his life. "Boy Scouts taught me academic skills, self-confidence, leadership, and citizenship. It's a program with a vision to guide boys into great men."

As Roy absorbed the stories, he expressed his desire to become a scout. Sonny, promising to explore the possibilities after Roy's 10th birthday, smiled, recognizing the potential for new adventures and shared experiences between father and son.

The sun continued its dance on the lake, casting reflections on the water of shared narratives woven tighter, creating memories that would endure a lifetime.

Echoes of a Patriarch's Legacy

As the noon sun reached its peak, Sonny skillfully guided the boat into a shady grove, a peaceful haven where he and Roy could enjoy the sandwiches Marsha had prepared for lunch. Their fishing lines remained idle, a testament to their yet unfulfilled fishing aspirations. Roy welcomed the break from the relentless sun, savoring the tranquility of the moment.

Sensing the right time to delve into a deeper chapter of his life, Sonny extended an invitation to Roy. "Son, I've shared a lot about my childhood. Do you have any lingering questions? Anything you'd like to know more about?"

Roy, reflecting on Granny's stories about Sonny's close-knit friendships that doubled as family, wanted to explore the dynamics of home life. He inquired, "Dad, can you tell me more about your time at home, especially with Poppa White?"

Joy gleaming in Sonny's eyes, he began to paint a vivid picture of Elzie White, his grandfather, the true patriarch of their family.

The Making of a Good Man

"Elzie White was the ultimate provider, a man of kindness who cared for us and the community. He loved music, camping, and adventure."

Sonny shared anecdotes of Poppa White's good looks, his daily ritual of tending to the garden, and his prowess in hunting and fishing. Laughter echoed as Sonny revealed his picky eating habits, a trait inherited from his childhood. "I passed on dishes like turtle soup because I had a pet turtle, but Poppa White teased me, saying I'd be a dry cereal lover when I grew up. And you know what? He was right."

"Your great grandparents had the farm to table or more appropriately **_wild_** to table down to a science: Poppa White caught, and Granny cooked every animal he caught. We had squirrels, chickens, rabbits, turtles, fish—I think we even ate wild birds unbeknownst to us. He shot everything that had meat potential, and he didn't necessarily wait until he was out hunting. If he was sitting in the chair and spotted an animal in the yard, he'd open the back door and shoot it from the inside of the house."

Roy, intrigued, asked about Sonny's early experiences with shooting. "Did you learn to shoot from Poppa White?"

Amused, Sonny confessed, "Despite finding Poppa White's hunting skills amusing, I was never fond of killing animals."

Poppa White's love for baseball also entered the narrative, becoming an unintended family bonding activity. Sonny chuckled, recalling his attempts to switch the channel to cartoons when Poppa White dozed off during baseball games.

"As I've reflected on Poppa White's life, many things I enjoy today stem from his influence," Sonny shared. "My love for RV trips, color preferences, and watches are all traces of Poppa White's enduring impact."

However, Sonny shifted the tone, recounting a lesson learned in retrospect, a tale of missed opportunities and unappreciated blessings. "Roy, sometimes when you're blessed with a loving family, you may lose sight of how much you need to show them appreciation."

Sonny revealed a poignant moment post-college graduation when he failed to serve Poppa White with the gratitude he deserved. Roy listened as Sonny shared the weight of regret he carried for his last encounter with his grandfather.

"Post-college graduation, I drove Granny and Poppa White to South Carolina for a family

The Making of a Good Man

gathering. While there, attending a huge fish fry at my cousin's house, my aunt asked me to fix Poppa White's plate. At the time, I was used to watching all the women fix the men's plates, so I was wondering why I had to fix it.

"Reluctantly, I fixed Poppa White's plate, but I didn't do it out of a place of love. I did it because I was asked to do it, but my attitude was one of an entitled man who couldn't grasp what an honor it was to serve his Poppa—especially after he'd spent most of his life faithfully serving me.

"Sadly, this was the last opportunity I had to serve Poppa White. In true Poppa White form, he was unphased by my disposition. I will always remember the smile on his face when I gave him his plate."

Roy, understanding the lesson, hugged his dad tightly. In that silent embrace, a promise lingered—a commitment from Roy to honor Poppa White's legacy by serving others with love. The echoes of a patriarch's lessons resonated, weaving into the tapestry of their shared stories on the peaceful lake.

Tapestry Woven with Generations of Love

The noon sun bathed the lake in golden hues as Sonny and Roy, satiated from their lunch, ventured back into the rippling waters with renewed hope for a fruitful catch. The remnants of their meal secured, Sonny, mindful of Roy's curiosity about his family, steered the conversation toward his childhood influencers.

"Most of my childhood memories are intertwined with family and friends who became family," Sonny mused, the boat gently gliding over the lake's surface. "From the daily routines with Granny and Poppa White to fishing trips with Mom, playtime with Stacey, and outings with Reverend Leo, family has always been at the center of my experiences."

Having delved into the rich tapestry of his grandfather's influence, Sonny felt it fitting to continue the narrative with his father, who was also named Roy.

"When my dad returned from serving in the Army in Vietnam," Sonny began, the memories resurfacing, "he'd pick me up from Granny's, and our first stop was always McDonald's—every kid's favorite restaurant." He paused, a fond smile playing on his lips. "Then we'd go from house to house to visit my cousins on the way home from camp. Dad knew everyone, and everyone knew him."

Sonny's voice carried a warmth as he described his father's vibrant personality. "All the way home, people would blow their horns, yelling, 'Hey, Roy!' and he'd make it a point to stop and speak. Dad was, and still is, the epitome of a people person. He found joy in serving others, checking on the neighborhood elderly, offering free household repairs, ensuring our community was cared for."

Turning to Roy, Sonny took a deep breath, as if preparing to share something significant. "Roy," Sonny began, his voice soft but filled with conviction, "do you know what our name means?"

Roy furrowed his brow, intrigued by the question. "What do you mean, Dad?"

"Well," Sonny explained, "our name, Roy, it's not just a name. It's a title, a legacy that stretches back through generations."

Roy's interest piqued, leaning in to listen more intently.

"Roy," Sonny continued, "it means 'king.' It's a name that carries with it a sense of strength, leadership, and responsibility."

Roy's eyes widened in surprise. "Really? I had no idea."

"Yes," Sonny affirmed, a proud smile spreading across his face. "And you, my son, are named after both your grandfather and me. Three generations of Roys, each carrying the weight of that name, each striving to live up to its meaning."

Young Roy sat back, letting the significance of his name sink in. He felt a sense of pride swelling within him, knowing that he was part of a lineage of kings, tasked with upholding the honor and dignity associated with his name.

"As you grow older, Roy," Sonny said, placing a hand on his son's shoulder, "remember the legacy you carry. Be proud of who you are and the name you bear."

Roy nodded, a newfound sense of purpose filling his heart. "I will, Dad. I'll do my best to live up to the name Roy, to be a king in my own right."

As the boat gently rocked, Sonny redirected his narrative to his childhood summer routines with his Dad. "During the summer, we'd go around Flint and Mt. Morris, house to house, checking on family members and friends. Poppa

White laid the foundation, and Dad reinforced how I eventually grew to genuinely care for others. My dad freely gave his resources, time, and talents, and I grew to do the same."

Roy listened attentively, captivated by the stories that painted a picture of his grandfather's legacy and the enduring influence of his father. The lake, their backdrop, mirrored the reflections of a generational love that transcended time. With each shared memory, Sonny not only unveiled the rich heritage Roy came from but also imparted the essence of compassion and community that had been woven into the fabric of their family's history.

The boat, now gliding toward the heart of the lake, carried not only father and son but also the echoes of a love that extended beyond bloodlines—a love rooted in selfless service and genuine care for others.

Summer Tale of Camp, Crushes, and Catches

Sonny's summer days unfolded in a vibrant tapestry of youthful adventures, and for him, those days spent with his dad were nothing short of magical. As the sun painted the sky with warm hues, Sonny regaled Roy with tales of summer escapades that unfolded at a bustling day camp.

"I spent most of my summer days with my dad, and I loved it!" Sonny began, steering the boat through the tranquil waters, setting the stage for a story that would whisk them back to the bygone days of childhood. "While he worked on weekdays, I attended a summer day camp near Connie's house."

As Sonny spoke, the boat gently rocked, mirroring the rhythm of his nostalgic recollections. "Day camp was a blast! A place where kids from all over the city could come together for games, food, and endless interactions. Among the many games we played, two stood out as my favorites—Chase and Hide and Go Seek."

He chuckled, the memories unfolding like a cherished photo album. "Most of my cousins around my age attended, too. I spent my time talking and playing with my cousin Cheryl and her friend Jackie. It made the summer days vibrant and productive."

Roy's curiosity piqued, and he interrupted, "Dad, did you have a girlfriend at camp?"

A mischievous glint sparkled in Sonny's eyes. "Well, there were a couple of girls. Jackie had a crush on me, but I met another girl, my Twin, named Yushika. We shared the same birthday, September 29th. I thought she was the cutest girl there."

Roy, eager for more details, inquired, "Did you ask her to be your girlfriend?"

Sonny's laughter resonated across the water. "You know, things were different back then. I didn't ask her officially, but we spent a lot of time together. Every day, I looked forward to seeing if my Twin was there. She even gave me a picture of herself, which I still have."

Though Sonny and Yushika were fond of each other, he and Jackie spent the most time together. Years later, Sonny found out Jackie had threatened to fight Yushika if she tried to be his girlfriend. "Youthful crush drama," Sonny chuckled, "but to this day when we have the opportunity to connect, it's all love."

Interrupting the trip down memory lane, Roy, with youthful enthusiasm, announced, "Dad, I think I caught one!"

Excitement surged through the boat as they worked together to reel in their elusive catch, a brief interruption to their otherwise fish-less day.

Unperturbed, they pledged to linger a little longer, hoping the lake would yield its treasures before the sun dipped below the horizon. And as the stories unfolded, father and son found themselves immersed not only in the pursuit of fish but also in the timeless tales of camp, childhood crushes, and the enduring laughter of shared memories.

The Mouse, the Bond, and the Promise

As the sun dipped lower over the serene lake, casting a warm glow on the water, Sonny found himself reminiscing about the elusive catches that didn't involve fish. Turning to his son Roy, who sat beside him in the boat, he chuckled, "Son, I can't believe we haven't caught anything yet. But speaking of catching things with a fishing pole, this reminds me of the time my friend Shawn and I tried to catch a mouse with one."

Roy's eyes widened in surprise, "A mouse? With a fishing pole?"

"Yes, son, crazy, I know," Sonny admitted with a grin, diving into a tale from his mischievous childhood. "On weekends, Shawn would spend the night. We, along with my uncle Lester, would stay up all night playing electric football, roughhousing, and jumping on the bed."

The boat gently rocked as Sonny transported them back to those lively nights. "One night, we kept hearing this noise in the hall closet. We figured it was a mouse—a mouse we were determined to catch. My tool of choice? A fishing pole."

Roy, clearly intrigued, interrupted, "A fishing pole for a mouse? How did that work?!"

"Believe it or not, Shawn went along with it." Sonny chuckled. "I had caught a turtle with a fishing pole before, so catching a mouse seemed like a plausible idea."

Roy laughed. "And did it work?"

Armed with determination, cheese, and a fishing pole, Sonny and Shawn devised a plan. They strategically placed the bait by the closet door, hid, and waited. True to their expectations, the mouse seized the cheese, and Sonny, using his fishing skills, snared the mouse like a fish on a line.

Roy, still incredulous, exclaimed, "You're making this up, Dad!"

"Nope, this really happened. We were two determined boys who weren't afraid to think outside the box," Sonny affirmed.

"What did you do with the mouse?"

"Unlike the turtle, we didn't want it to bite us, so we took it outside, cut the line, and off it ran with the hook. It was quite a sight," Sonny replied, savoring the memory.

Eager for more details, Roy inquired about Lester, the missing link in this particular adventure. Sonny explained that Lester, his uncle of the same age, was a vital part of their trio. As they played cops and robbers, shared summer nights, and reveled in their unspoken dream of becoming policemen, Lester had left an indelible mark on Sonny's childhood.

"One weekend during our usual bed jump-a-thons, Lester jumped too far, and both his feet went through the wall," Sonny continued, a mischievous twinkle in his eye. "When my mom heard the noise, she ran into the room, shouting, 'Who put this hole in the wall?' I pointed at Lester, and he pointed at me. To this day, Lester has never admitted to kicking the hole in the wall."

Sonny shared how Lester grew up to be a Naval man, a skilled boiler technician in the U.S. Navy. Leaving the Navy, he worked in the hospital system and became deeply involved in his community, embodying the lessons of positive role models he learned from in his youth.

"Lester is stern and has high expectations for the kids he mentors because he wants them to achieve their fullest potential," Sonny proudly declared. "Some of the kids he has coached have gone on to the NFL. He coaches basketball and football and is also involved in baseball."

As the boat gently floated on the tranquil lake, the tales of fishing poles, mice, and lifelong friendships wove a colorful narrative, painting a vivid picture of Sonny's spirited and adventurous youth.

The Art of Protection

As the sun dipped below the horizon, casting a warm, orange glow over the lake, Roy and Sonny decided it was time to call it a day. Sonny, eager to impart more of his life's stories and lessons, began to recount the tales of his siblings as they strolled back to the house.

Sonny's voice carried the sentimentality of childhood bonds and the unique dynamics among his five sisters and brother. He spoke of Tootie, the eldest, who had been his fiercest protector during their youth. A defender in the game of thumps, she would take all the pain intended for him, solidifying their unbreakable bond of sibling love.

"Tootie was my caretaker when Mom wasn't around," Sonny reminisced. "We would fight for the position of who's the leader in Mom's absence. But we both knew it was all in love. When I was younger, she always had the upper hand, but as I grew, my masculine strength was no match for her. Still, our bond was like no other. She was truly the epitome of what a big sister should be.

"Tootie grew up to be a phlebotomist, working for the Red Cross," Sonny explained. "She also opened her first business on South Saginaw Street with her business partner, Almeta. The business was called Beauty Blessings and Apparel. I still remember reading the newspaper article feature of her business."

Sonny continued, introducing each sibling with honor. Meice, the consummate organizer, maternal figure, and now banker, was his inseparable companion. "Just two years younger than me, Meice and I did everything together: we ran track, hung out, broke curfew, and faced punishment together. We were so close I escorted her to her senior prom."

"Pooh Bear wanted in on our bond, so she joined the track team, too, but she could not stand being mothered by Meice. However, as we grew, our duo became a trio—Pooh Bear became an equal part of our sibling unit. Today, she's an international author, writing stories that have captivated readers worldwide."

Roy, captivated by the tales of familial bonds, listened intently as Sonny continued to recount each sibling's journey.

As he continued, Sonny's voice brimmed with affection. "Then there was Kimmy, the one who could do no wrong in Mom's eyes. Tootie and I used to exchange knowing looks whenever Kimmy talked back to Mom, fully expecting her to get disciplined. But she had a knack for getting away with it."

"Kim was highly intelligent, always thinking of new ways to make money," Sonny explained. "She'd administer shots to animals in the neighborhood, barter with the grocery store owner for discount dog food, and then resell it to her friends. She was a born hustler, and it didn't stop there. Kim grew up to become a certified entrepreneur, shaping marijuana laws in Michigan as the first Black female business owner of a legalized marijuana facility."

Roy's eyes widened in amazement. "That's incredible, Dad."

Sonny nodded, his smile widening. "And your aunt Venus, she was a firecracker! Waking her up for school was a daily struggle; she just couldn't seem to get out of bed in the morning. Venus was Dad's favorite. We used to tease her a lot, but deep down, we cherished her. She had this special bond with Dad that none of us could compete with."

Roy smiled, picturing a young version of his aunt Venus in his mind. "Aunt Venus sounds like she was a character."

Sonny laughed, nodding in agreement. "Oh, she definitely was! Today, she's a poet and entrepreneur. And finally, there's Damien, the baby boy, with his impeccable style and swagger. He was quieter than the rest of us, but no less loved. We spoiled him rotten, and he wore that swag like a badge of honor. Now, seeing him successful in his career at Ford Motors, I can't help but feel proud of the man he's become."

Reflecting on their bond, Sonny's voice softened with emotion, "Growing up with my siblings shaped each of us in unique ways. Despite the teasing and the fights, the love we shared was undeniable. I may not have always been the best big brother, but I loved them fiercely, and I still do. They're my family, my rock, and I'm grateful for every moment we've shared together. They're the reason I am who I am today. One of the biggest lessons your aunts and uncle taught me was how to be a protector."

Roy, curious, asked, "How did they teach you that?"

"As the oldest son," Sonny began, "I learned from Poppa White and my dad the importance of being there for my mom and sisters. Simple gestures like opening doors and walking on the outside of the sidewalk near the street may seem small, but they communicated a desire to make the women in my life feel safe and protected."

Roy crooked his head to the side, perplexed. "What's the point of walking on the outside of the sidewalk?"

Sonny smiled, recognizing an opportunity for an age-old lesson. "In the event a vehicle should veer off the road, you'd be there to protect the woman you're walking with."

Roy, contemplating the responsibility, voiced his concern. "But, Dad, who's gonna protect you and me?"

Sonny responded with a reassuring smile. "God is always going to protect us."

Roy, seeking clarity, asked a deeper question, "Why can't God protect them in the same way, too?"

Sonny, ever the guide and mentor, explained, "God has prepared you to serve the women in your life in this way. While He is the ultimate protector, He gives us the desire to partner with Him to ensure His children are protected. As you continue on this quest to learn what it takes to be a good man, God will enable you to practice what it means to protect the women in your life so much so that you'll begin doing so innately."

Roy, touched by his father's affection for his siblings, felt a pang of longing as he spoke. "Dad, it's no secret I've always wanted a brother or sister... I think my reason has been mostly to have someone to play with, but I never really thought about how having a brother or sister could affect my character."

Sonny paused, his gaze thoughtful as he considered his son's words. "Son, you may not have experienced some of the lessons I've learned from my siblings growing up, but you'll learn brothers and sisters aren't always part of your bloodline." Hearing this, Roy nodded in agreement, remembering what Granny had shared about his dad's brotherly bond with PJ, Rodney, Joe Joe, Shawn, and Juan. The idea of having that kind of connection tugged at Roy's heartstrings.

Then, a spark of realization crossed Sonny's face. "You know what, Roy? How about we invite some of your cousins over for the weekend?"

Roy's eyes lit up with excitement. "Really? That would be awesome!"

Sonny smiled, his plan forming. "Yeah. We'll have five of your cousins spend the weekend with us. It'll be like having siblings around, and you can see what it's like to share the house with family. I know how much you enjoy spending time with Zyon."

Roy grinned from ear to ear. The prospect of having his cousins over filled him with anticipation. "That sounds amazing, Dad! I can't wait!"

Sonny nodded, feeling a sense of satisfaction at the idea. "Great! And you know, this could become a regular thing. Granny always taught me the importance of bonding with family, and I think it's time we pass that down to you."

Roy nodded eagerly, already envisioning the fun times ahead with his cousins. "I'm all for it, Dad. And I'll be sure to show them a good time."

Sonny clapped a hand on Roy's shoulder, his heart full with the thought of creating new memories with his son and their extended family. "I know you will, son. I believe you'll develop a bond with your cousins just like I did with my siblings."

The evening settled around them, the lake mirroring the colors of the setting sun, as the lessons of family, protection, and love continued to weave their way through generations.

A Legacy of Love: From Fishing Tales to Love Stories

As the sun dipped below the horizon, Sonny and Roy made their way home, their hearts lightened by a day filled with fishing and bonding. Little did they know that the evening held more surprises for them.

When they entered the house, the warm aroma of Roy's favorite, fried chicken, welcomed them. Marsha and Granny were found relaxing in the living room. The day seemed to unfold like a perfectly scripted family gathering.

Marsha, ever the nurturing mother, inquired, "So, what'd you catch?"

Roy and Sonny exchanged glances and shook their heads, indicating an empty fish basket.

Unfazed, Marsha smiled. "Well, knowing how hard you were working, I thought it only fitting to make your favorite!"

Ecstatic, Roy exclaimed, "Mom, you're the BEST!" He rushed to wash his hands, eager to join the family at the dinner table.

The Making of a Good Man

As they settled in, Granny and Marsha, knowing the purpose behind the fishing trip, prompted Roy to share his newfound wisdom. Amidst stories of childhood and embedded lessons, Roy acknowledged the influence of family in shaping a person's character.

Marsha, recognizing Sonny as the best-equipped storyteller, asserted, "Roy, I know you asked me to explain what it takes to become a good man, but I'm so glad your dad's here to outline and model what it takes to be a good man. We're so fortunate to reap the benefits."

Encouraged by the family's interest, Sonny assured Roy that there was more to tell. Even though he knew he'd have a lifetime of opportunities to share life lessons with his son, given Roy's question, he was determined to spend this weekend crystallizing the events that had shaped his character.

Interrupting his thoughts, Roy posed a new question, "Dad, I know you've only gotten through telling me about your childhood, but can you tell me about you and mom? When did you meet her? How did she know you were a good man? I often hear her telling Aunt Sandra you're a good man. How did she come to see you this way?"

Sonny, glancing at Marsha with a humbled smile, deferred to his wife. Marsha, with equal humility, invited Sonny to share their love story. "Roy, would you like to do the honors?"

"Well, son," Sonny began, "as much as I thought I was a good man, my actions told a truer story."

Sonny took a trip down memory lane, describing his college days when he caught Marsha's eye through his exemplary conduct. Dressed impeccably, engaging with everyone on campus, and displaying discipline in his studies, Sonny attracted like-minded individuals.

"We were friends for a couple of months," Sonny continued. "I would walk her to class, carry her books, and we spent time together with our group of friends."

Nonetheless, though they could see a future with each other, Marsha was a senior who had her eyes set on a career beyond the limits of Ohio, and Sonny had just begun his college career. As a result, they made the decision to part ways.

However, as fate would have it, 14 years after their separation, their paths were realigned through mutual friends in Columbia, SC.

Hearing this, Roy's eyes widened with awe at the realization of how miraculous it was for his parents to find themselves back to each other through distance and time.

They worked together at the YMCA, becoming personal trainers. Together, they trained a group of women called Women on Weights, witnessing their transformation into a fit and active community. Sonny recollected their success as a team, highlighting the power of collaboration.

Their rekindled friendship deepened into a caring relationship. They shared their favorite snacks, became successful personal trainers, and enjoyed various social events together. Marsha appreciated Sonny's kind demeanor and chivalry.

Sonny, now animated by the memories, spoke of their early dates, monthly flowers, sweet notes, and romantic gestures. Roy listened wide-eyed, captivated by his parents' love story.

"After two years of courtship," Sonny continued, "I knew Marsha was and will forever be the queen in my life. So, I planned my proposal."

He recounted the horse and carriage ride through downtown, the surprise proposal at the State Capital, and the celebration with friends afterward.

Marsha added, "We dated for about two years, and the things I saw your dad do during our courtship let me know he was a good man. He would buy me flowers every month, leave sweet notes, and plan thoughtful surprises. He treated me with kindness, and I saw how he treated everyone around him."

As Roy absorbed this love story, Sonny concluded, "This is how your mom and I became husband and wife. This is how we set the foundation for you so you will become a good man by the things you see me do for your mom, as well as what we do with and for each other."

While preparing for bed, grateful thoughts filled Roy's mind. He pondered on the lessons of the day, the love his parents shared, and the foundations laid for his future.

Tucking Roy in, Sonny added one final piece of advice. "One day, son, you will find a young lady you are interested in, and I want you to treat her well. Treat everyone well, not for what you may get in return, but because it's the right thing to do."

The echoes of his father's words lingered as Roy embraced the dreams of a promising future shaped by the love, kindness, and guidance of his remarkable family.

A Sunday Serenade of Stories

The next morning bathed the Rogers household in the soft glow of dawn, and Roy, filled with anticipation, rose eager to uncover more tales from his father's past. The events of the fishing trip and the revelation of his parents' love story lingered in the air. However, Roy was aware that the day held a sacred rhythm, and church was the first note in the family's Sunday melody.

As they made their way to church in the family car, a familiar sense of comfort enveloped Roy. The rhythmic hum of the engine seemed to sync with his own heartbeat. The vibrant sun painted the sky with hues of gold and coral, signaling the dawn of another Sunday in their community.

Recollections from the previous day's stories, especially Granny's humorous anecdotes, played in Roy's mind like a cherished melody. He couldn't help but chuckle at the thought of his dad, attending church during his younger years to catch a glimpse of the girls, particularly with his friend PJ in tow.

The family's rich history seemed to be a tapestry woven with threads of love, laughter, and a touch of mischievousness.

During the drive, Sonny, in a reflective mood, delved into the memories of his elementary school years. The stories painted a vivid picture of a time when Sonny, much like Roy, reveled in both the joys of summer and the pleasures of education.

"I enjoyed the summers, but I also enjoyed school," Sonny began, his voice carrying the warmth of nostalgia. "I learned from other kids that my elementary school was different from theirs. Public schools had different programs of study based on where you lived. Some programs were not equipped to teach students as well as others, due to limited resources.

"I was fortunate to have the education I received in my formative years." A sense of gratitude evident filled his tone. "Based on what I've shared thus far, it's no secret that I enjoyed playing as much as you do, Roy, but I also enjoyed learning new things."

The car became a vessel of shared memories, with Sonny revealing his parents' commitment to his intellectual growth. "My parents made sure I had every encyclopedia you could think of," he added, emphasizing the value placed on knowledge. "Being smart was a big deal for me and my friends. Even though sometimes we were called nerds, I grew to like the term. Being a nerd meant I was different, not trying to be like everyone else. I stood out."

Roy, attentively listening, marveled at the contrast of educational experiences between schools during his dad's youth and his own school. He pondered the significance of the privileges his dad enjoyed, thanks to his parents' dedication to making sure Sonny attended schools with enriched learning environments.

As Sonny painted a picture of his younger self, Roy glimpsed the vibrant, multifaceted personality of his father. Sonny concluded with a subtle satisfaction, "I guess you could say I was well-liked, funny, and smart, but not necessarily in that order."

Roy smiled, contemplating the significance of his dad's journey from a playful, intellectually curious child to the wise and caring man he knew today. The car continued its journey through the quiet streets, carrying a family bound by stories, shared laughter, and the promise of another Sunday morning in the embrace of their community and faith.

PHASE TWO

Sunday Table Talks

As the aroma of Marsha's culinary prowess filled the air, the Rogers family gathered around the polished dining table, ready to savor their cherished Sunday lunch. Each dish held the promise of comfort and tradition. With a little assistance from Granny, Marsha had prepared a feast fit for royalty: blackened salmon, collard greens, mashed potatoes, macaroni and cheese, and to top it all off, a mouthwatering peach cobbler accompanied by a side of chocolate chip cookies, Roy's absolute favorite.

Seated around the formal dining table, the family dug into the delectable spread, their taste buds dancing with each flavorful bite. It was a time-honored tradition, cherished by all.

Amid this culinary delight, Sonny felt compelled to continue sharing pieces of his upbringing with his son; so, with a wistful gleam in his eyes, he cleared his throat, capturing the attention of his eager audience.

"Roy," Sonny began, his voice rich with reminiscence, "last night, I ended the day with our love story, but if you'd indulge me, I'd like to take you back to my preteen years, specifically my promotion to junior high school in Mt. Morris, Michigan."

Roy's curiosity piqued, he nodded eagerly, ready to delve back into his father's past.

"At Summit Jr. High, I was the new kid, trying to find my place," Sonny recounted, his words painting a vivid picture of his early struggles to fit in. "But then I met Joe."

Joe, the epitome of popularity and athleticism, initially clashed with Sonny in a whirlwind of competition. "We were like two bulls in a pen." Sonny chuckled. "We were highly competitive and determined to prove we could outdo each other. However, his backflipping abilities far exceeded mine, but instead of holding this advantage over my head, Joe taught me how to do a backflip over a huge snowball we'd made across the street from my house. After that exchange, Joe and I were inseparable."

Tickled, Sonny continued. "One of our favorite pastimes was slap boxing. During each match, we'd declare, 'I'm the best,' panning each other every step of the way. But when it was all over, we knew it was all fun."

"What's panning?" Roy interrupted, his interest piqued.

Sonny grinned. "It's basically making fun of each other. I guess you'd call it trash talking, but all in fun."

"You were a trash talker, Dad?!" Roy retorted. "I can't see you trash talkin' anyone."

Granny confirmed that Sonny was a huge trash talker. "It was what he and his friends and cousins did for sport all day long."

Amidst their laughter, Sonny paused, his expression turning thoughtful. "In retrospect," he mused, "panning taught us resilience and quick wittedness, skills that have served me well throughout my life."

While Sonny maintained good grades, he and his friends often found themselves in after school detention for passing comedic self-portraits during class.

Sonny's tales of mischief and friendships continued. "Detention wasn't all bad," he confessed to Roy's surprise.

Roy seized the opportunity, teasing his dad about his past misdeeds. "So, does that mean I get a pass if I ever find myself in detention?"

The Making of a Good Man

At which point, Marsha and Granny glanced at each other as if to say, "I'm glad I don't have to answer this one, but let's see how Sonny addresses this."

Sonny's response was measured, filled with parental wisdom and understanding. "Son, at 12 and, quite honestly, even as an adult, I have not always made the best decisions, but my hope is that you'll learn from my mistakes." His gaze toward Roy was unwavering, "I hope that you'd want to tell us if you're ever in trouble. Would we discipline you? Most likely, but the logic behind our decision to do so is so that you'd avoid making the same poor decision again."

As the weight of this teachable moment filled the room and Roy's smirk faltered, the family shared a moment of connection and understanding. And as they lingered around the table, basking in the warmth of shared memories, they knew that these Sunday table talks were more than just a meal—they were a testament to the bonds that held them together, now and always.

Trails of Reflection

After the hearty Sunday lunch, Sonny and Roy decided to trade their fishing rods for hiking boots, venturing into the backwoods of their neighborhood. As they trekked along the marked trail, surrounded by towering trees and the gentle sounds of nature, Sonny resumed unveiling the tales of his youth.

"During one of my stints in detention," Sonny began, his voice carrying the weight of memories, "I noticed Erica sitting alone in a corner. She lived in the corner house of our neighborhood.

"I thought she was cute and wanted to befriend her, but her cousin had other ideas. Every time I'd go outside, I'd see Erica and her cousin playing. I wanted to introduce myself, but I'd always hear Erica's cousin taunting me from way down the street, yelling, 'Hey Bucky!'"

Roy's brow furrowed in confusion. "Why'd she call you Bucky?"

Sonny chuckled softly, his laughter echoing through the woods. "Because of my big front teeth," he explained, a wistful smile playing on his lips. "One day, she even left a toothbrush and some dentures in my mailbox."

Roy's sympathy was evident as he processed his father's encounter with Erica's cousin. "That's tough, Dad," he murmured.

Sonny nodded, his gaze distant yet thoughtful. "I know, right? I'd like to tell you my feelings weren't hurt, but they were. I never knew why she didn't like me, but I never let it stop me from being kind to them."

As they continued their hike, Sonny reflected on the importance of kindness, even in the face of adversity. "Never treat people poorly just because they mistreat you," he advised, his words a testament to his upbringing.

Despite Erica's cousin's animosity, Sonny chose to respond with kindness, refusing to let her actions define his character. "You know, I never actually had the chance to talk to Erica nor her cousin," he mused, a hint of disbelief tingeing his voice, "but to this day, I still wonder why her cousin picked on me."

As the trees shielded them from the sun-scorched trail, their hearts were filled with a newfound appreciation for the trails of reflection that life often presents. Walking in companionable silence, Roy honored his dad's vulnerability, which validated Sonny's humanity. These moments were the makings of an unbreakable father-son bond.

A First Crush Memory

As the sun dipped lower in the sky, casting long shadows across the forest floor, Sonny's reminiscences continued, his voice filled with a wistful warmth.

"Unlike Erica's cousin, the other girls always liked me because of my big afro," Sonny recounted with a chuckle. "They loved braiding my hair."

Roy listened attentively, a smile tugging at the corners of his lips as his father's tale unfolded.

"In junior high, I met my first girlfriend," Sonny continued, his voice tinged with fondness. "I called her Yoda."

Roy's eyebrows shot up in surprise. "Yoda?! Did she look like the Jedi Master in *Star Wars*?"

Chuckling with a reminiscent twinkle in his eye, Sonny explained, "No, son. It was my abbreviation for her name, Yalonda. She didn't like it much, but she liked me."

Yalonda, or Yoda as Sonny affectionately called her, was a beacon of beauty and intelligence at Summit Jr. High. "She was the prettiest girl at school," Sonny said. "Smart, pretty, and athletic. A true junior high school queen who later became the high school queen."

As Sonny recounted the memories of his teenage years, Roy leaned in closer, captivated by the unfolding.

"One day, as we walked home from school, Yoda surprised me with my first kiss," Sonny revealed, a soft smile playing on his lips. "And believe it or not, it happened right in front of Erica's house."

Roy's eyes widened with curiosity. "Did Erica see y'all?"

Sonny shook his head, a hint of disappointment flickering across his features. "No, she and her cousin weren't outside."

Despite the missed opportunity to flaunt his newfound romance, Sonny's affection for Yoda only grew stronger with time. "From that day on, I couldn't stop thinking about her," he confessed, his voice laced with a sense of longing.

As Roy listened to his father's tale of young love, his heart was touched by the enduring memory of Sonny's first crush.

Lessons Learned on the Block

Continuing their journey through the woods, the echoes of Sonny's past mingled with the rustling of leaves. Roy continued listening intently, clinging to his father's every word.

"Making new friends was exciting," Sonny said, a hint of nostalgia coloring his voice. "On our street, there was Reggie, Daryl, Fat Boy (who was ironically very skinny), Todd, Nick, Daniel, and my cousin. We had quite a crew."

The memories of their childhood antics flickered vibrantly in Sonny's mind as he recounted the simple joys of street play. "When school was out, we'd play from sunup 'til sundown, but when the streetlights came on, I had to go home," Sonny explained. "Mom was strict about curfew, and for good reason, but I hated having a curfew because most of my friends didn't have one."

Roy nodded in understanding, absorbing the lessons his father was reluctant to embrace. "I can imagine how frustrating it must have been," he mused.

Sonny's eyes sparkled with mischief as he recalled an audacious stunt from his youth. "One day, I decided to take matters into my own hands and disable the streetlight. I got my dad's BB gun and shot the streetlights out. That night when it got late the streetlights didn't come on, so I was able to stay out way past my curfew. I thought this idea was genius! No streetlights meant no curfew—right?" he confessed, a mischievous grin playing on his lips.

Roy's eyes widened in disbelief. "You literally shot the streetlights out?"

Sonny chuckled, shaking his head at his own audacity. "I thought I was being clever, but I soon learned that my selfish decision had grave consequences."

Roy nodded solemnly, understanding the weight of his father's words. "After you told me about shooting the streetlights out, I couldn't help but wonder how Grandma knew it was you."

Sonny sighed, his expression softening. "You're right, son. Grandma didn't miss anything. She was probably in the window watching for me to head into the house. But this time, I told on myself."

Roy's eyebrows shot up. "You confessed?"

Sonny nodded. "Integrity at a young age. I couldn't keep the guilt inside. I went straight to her and confessed I shot the lights out. Your grandma made me go outside and clean up all the glass so no one got hurt."

The gravity of Sonny's lesson hung heavy in the air as he continued his tale. "That night, I learned the hard way that poor decisions come with repercussions," he admitted, his voice laced with ruefulness. "While this offense was much more serious than serving detention for passing comedic self-portraits in class, the lesson here is the same: in life, we will be held responsible for our actions, so choose wisely, son.

"I hated disappointing my parents," Sonny lamented, "so on top of receiving their punishment, I punished myself with the burden of my guilt."

Despite this setback, Sonny found solace in the friendship he forged with Reggie. "Reggie became my closest friend," Sonny revealed. "We bonded over fixing bikes, and he taught me a lot."

Roy listened with rapt attention as his father recounted the adventures he shared with Reggie, their laughter echoing through the neighborhood as they rode their bikes for hours on end.

In the days following the streetlight incident, Sonny's "playground" was limited to a one-mile radius. "But when my mom finally gave me permission to ride my bike to Meijers (which was our Walmart) with Reggie, it felt like I'd been given a second chance," Sonny concluded, a sense of gratitude warming his heart. "Her 'yes' was a sign of forgiveness and trust, and I wasn't about to let her down again."

Lessons in Responsibility and Financial Wisdom

As Sonny and Roy trekked through the wooded trail, the conversation seamlessly shifted to a more practical topic—Roy's allowance.

"Wait a second, Dad, you know what today is, right?" Roy interjected, a hint of excitement in his voice.

Sonny chuckled, amused by his son's abrupt interjection. "Yes, it's Sunday. What does that mean to you?" he asked, playing along.

Roy's eyes lit up with anticipation. "It means I'm due my allowance!" he exclaimed eagerly.

Laughing warmly, Sonny gently said, "You're right, but since you don't have school tomorrow, I figured you won't need it until Tuesday."

Roy nodded in understanding before remembering another important detail. "That's right, tomorrow is MLK Day—does this mean we get to spend tomorrow together, too?"

"Absolutely!" Sonny affirmed, his heart swelling with warmth. "There's so much I want to share with you, and I realize we'll have a lifetime more of conversations. But I want to honor your quest to learn what it takes to become a good man, and the best way I can explain this is through the experiences that have shaped me into one."

Inviting Roy into a moment of reflection, Sonny continued, "I know I've shared a lot, but what are some things that stand out to you so far, Roy?"

Roy's mind buzzed with thoughts as he reflected on the stories his father had shared. "Well, Dad, from what you've shared so far, I'd say your experiences taught you to believe in yourself, face your fears, treat others the way you'd like to be treated, and take responsibility for your actions."

Pride swelled in Sonny's chest as he listened to his son's insightful observations. "Son, if you commit to living out these principles, it's likely you'll grow up to be a great man—even greater than I am."

"I'll do my best," Roy said, smiling up at his father.

"Now," Sonny said, rubbing Roy's shoulder, "back to the subject of allowances. I didn't have it as easy as you have it."

Their conversation then turned to Sonny's early financial lessons.

"I earned my allowance by working for the Caldwells. Mr. Caldwell was a hunter and a fisherman, and my job every week was to clean all his hunting dogs' kennels. My hard work earned me ten dollars every Friday." Noticing Roy's disbelief in what he had to do to earn his allowance, Sonny continued, "Ten dollars a week was a lot then, and I was sure to steward it well. Every week, I gave a dollar as an offering to the church, put seven dollars in the savings account my dad helped me open, spent a dollar on a grape soda and cookies (my fav), and used a dollar to play video games at the store."

As Sonny recounted his routine of earning, saving, and giving, Roy marveled at the responsible way his father managed his earnings.

"Did you actually have to go to the bank?" Roy asked, dubious at the thought of handling transactions without modern technology.

Sonny chuckled, shaking his head at the memory. "No, son. Most times, I asked my dad to put the money in my account for me. Back then we physically had to go to the bank to make transactions. Most people used cash, some checks, but we knew nothing about electronic transactions."

Stunned, Roy expressed, "Wow, Dad! You could've saved so much time if you had access to online banking."

Affirming his son's point, Sonny agreed, adding, "Though I didn't save time, the bigger takeaway here is I was saving money. Those seven dollars in the bank every week added up. Looking back, if I would have known a better way of saving my money so it could make money I would have. A savings account is a great way to store your money, but it's not the best way to make your money grow."

Roy's interest piqued further as Sonny explained his financial habits and the importance of making money work for you. "Is this why you have me put some of my savings in a special account?" Roy queried, eager to understand the rationale behind his father's guidance.

"Exactly, son," Sonny affirmed, a sense of pride evident in his voice. "Your money grows faster with investing in mutual funds. This is one effortless way to make your money make money for you."

As their hike continued, Roy absorbed every word, grateful for the invaluable lessons his father imparted—lessons that would guide him

The Making of a Good Man

not only in his financial decisions, but in his journey toward becoming a responsible, compassionate, and successful man.

Entrepreneurship and Financial Discipline

Sonny's entrepreneurial journey began when he delved into a new business opportunity that stemmed from his love of fishing and his knack for spotting potential ventures.

With enthusiasm, Sonny elaborated on his venture into the world of selling nightcrawlers, an endeavor that not only capitalized on his expertise in fishing bait, but also forged new friendships and business partnerships.

"I started selling Mr. Caldwell nightcrawlers," Sonny recounted. "At this age, I was digging for worms and making cups of worms for my mom because she loved to fish. I would always have her nightcrawlers ready. Then the idea of selling worms to the people in the neighborhood occurred to me."

Sonny's relationship with money and work was deeply influenced by his upbringing. Humbled, he continued, "Like you, Roy, I was fortunate to learn the value of a dollar from my dad at a very early age. I understood the connection between work and pay—these two exist on equal plains, for as much as one's willing to work, so he/she will earn."

Sonny continued, his eyes gleaming with nostalgia, "My friend Bill's family loved to fish, too, so his dad invented a device he called the worm finder. Inspired by my work ethic, he made one for me, too. It was actually a pole that released electric currents that traveled through the ground, causing the nightcrawlers to come to the surface."

Roy listened intently as Sonny described the ingenious worm finder, a device that revolutionized his worm-catching operation, making it more efficient and lucrative than ever before.

"The worm finder meant no more digging for me." Sonny chuckled, recalling the days of laboriously searching for nightcrawlers. "With the worm finder, I had nightcrawlers on demand. It was a game-changer."

As Sonny recounted his success in selling nightcrawlers to eager fishermen in the neighborhood, Roy marveled at his father's ingenuity and resourcefulness.

"So, you had your own business when you were in junior high school, Dad?" Roy exclaimed, impressed by his father's entrepreneurial spirit.

Sonny nodded proudly. "I sure did! I was an entrepreneur and didn't even know it!" He laughed, sharing Roy's amusement at the thought of his younger self peddling worms and nightcrawlers.

Roy grinned, envisioning his own future as a business owner. "Wow, Dad! I hope to have a business when I get to junior high, but I'm definitely not going to be selling worms and nightcrawlers," he quipped, eliciting laughter from both of them, given Roy's disdain for all creepy crawly things.

Encouraging his son's aspirations, Sonny offered guidance and support. "Son, I like how you're thinking. You don't have to wait until you're in junior high to start planning. I'll help you figure it out when the time comes."

Reflecting on his financial habits during his youth, Sonny emphasized the importance of financial discipline and smart work ethic. "I grossed $40 to $48 a week, so I averaged $160 to $192 a month. Each week, I'd tithed 10% to the church, put 50% in my savings account, shared some of the money with my siblings, and spent approximately 10% on myself. And I did this all throughout junior high school into high school.

"Exercising this financial discipline not only taught me the basic principles of managing money, but it also taught me that success is possible when you work smart," he explained, hopeful these lessons would resonate with his son.

As they continued their hike, Roy pondered upon his dad's values of hard work, responsibility, and pursuit of success with hopes that one day he, too, would embody similar attributes.

Elderly Treasures

As the sun cast its golden glow over the rugged terrain, this father and son duo continued their hike through the picturesque wilderness, their footsteps echoing against the tranquil backdrop of nature's symphony.

"Dad, you said you worked for the Caldwells. Did you work for his wife as well?" Roy's voice carried through the crisp mountain air, breaking the peaceful silence with his inquisitive tone.

"Well not quite...most of what I did was for Mr. Caldwell. However, I spent a lot of time with Mrs. Birdie who lived next to the Caldwells," Sonny replied, his words laced with the warmth of cherished memories.

As they navigated the winding trail, Sonny recounted the days he spent assisting Mrs. Birdie, his youthful acts of kindness unfolding like a cherished tale.

"I'd go to the store every week for Mrs. Birdie," Sonny continued. "She was about 80 years old, confined to a walker, so I took it upon myself to assist her in whatever way I could. I guess I modeled this behavior after my dad's example of caring for the elderly. Mrs. Birdie had an affinity for Burger King whoppers! So, when they were on sale, I was sure to take trips to Burger King on her behalf. Back then we could get like five whoppers for $10."

Roy listened intently as his father shared stories of Mrs. Birdie's fondness for Burger King whoppers, his laughter mingling with the rustle of leaves overhead.

"She'd eat five burgers at a time?!" Roy exclaimed, his eyes wide with surprise.

"She would freeze them," Sonny chuckled, his smile reflecting the fondness he felt for his dear neighbor. "Whenever I'd visit, we'd sit at the kitchen table, warm up a couple of whoppers, and much like the conversations we share, she'd share. Mrs. Birdie enjoyed my company, and oddly enough, I enjoyed spending time with her, too."

"Of course you did, Dad! We all know how much you love Burger King whoppers!" Roy jested. Equally entertained by Roy's witty observation, Sonny agreed in laughter, adding, "Very true son—very true!"

When they paused to catch their breath, Sonny's voice took on a reflective tone as he spoke of the profound impact Mrs. Birdie had on his life.

"I genuinely enjoyed my time with Mrs. Birdie. She'd seen a lot in her lifetime, so her stories were rich with lived experiences I'd only learned about from historical school references. She'd lived through the sharecropping era, Jim Crow, and so much more. As a result, she taught me so many lessons about navigating the woes of racism.

"She had endured so much cruelty, yet she was one of the sweetest elderly women I knew. I remember asking her, 'How can you be so kind despite the hatred you've experienced?' to which she responded, 'Love always overcomes hate.'

"Her presence left an indelible impression on me," Sonny confessed, his gaze drifting toward the distant horizon. "I remember thinking if she had lived through what she did and still managed to be kind, I have no reason to feel justified in repaying evil for evil."

"Dad, this reminds me of the story you told me about the kid who spat on you in elementary school," Roy interjected, drawing parallels between his father's past experiences and the lessons he had learned.

"You're exactly right, son," Sonny affirmed, his voice filled with wisdom born of experience. "Just as Granny worked to teach me this lesson, so, too, did Mrs. Birdie through the years."

Roy nodded in understanding, his admiration for his father's resilience evident in his gaze.

"Dad, I think it's really interesting that you spent so much time with elderly people—especially as a teenager," Roy noted.

"That's a keen observation, Roy," Sonny said, his pride in his son's perceptiveness shining through. "Conversations with the elderly have the potential to give you a glimpse into your future, to learn from their experiences so that you can ultimately make sound decisions."

Roy smiled, a sense of gratitude welling up within him as he contemplated the wisdom passed down from one generation to the next.

"So, is this like you asking me to learn from your mistakes?" Roy quipped, his tone light, yet sincere. "If so, does this make you an elder?"

Sonny nodded in agreement, his laughter mingling with the gentle rustle of leaves. "Yes, exactly. And who knows, one day you might find yourself in the same category as the 'elderly'—to your own children!"

Resuming their hike, father and son walked side by side, their hearts filled with the bond of love and an understanding that transcended generations. In the embrace of nature's embrace, they found solace and strength, united in their journey of growth and learning.

Trash Turned Treasure

As Sonny and Roy ambled along the hiking trail, the dense foliage provided a natural canopy overhead, filtering sunlight in dappling patterns onto the forest floor. Their conversation ebbed and flowed, weaving seamlessly with the rhythm of their footsteps.

"Mr. Buchanan, Mrs. Birdie's husband, was always on the move. Fishing was his favorite pastime, and one day, he took me with him. As you know, I was no stranger to fishing, but fishing with Mr. Buchanan was especially unique because it was the first time I fished from a boat."

Roy listened intently, absorbing his father's tales like a sponge, eager to glean wisdom from his experiences.

"It was unique to travel by boat to where the fish were. It made it easier to catch them."

As they reached a clearing in the trail, the shimmering waters of the lake stretched out before them like a tranquil oasis. Sonny suggested they take a moment to rest, and they settled onto a weathered wooden bench overlooking the picturesque vista.

Perched on the edge of the bench, Sonny delved into a poignant memory from his past, one that had left an indelible mark on his heart.

Amidst the tranquil beauty of the forest clearing, Sonny paused to reflect on a crucial lesson learned from Mr. Buchanan—a lesson not in words, but in actions. With quiet reverence, he recounted the story of the forgotten minibike, which ultimately became a symbol of the transformative power of generosity versus selfishness.

"Through Mr. Buchanan's unwitting guidance, I learned the value of letting go and embracing the joy of giving," Sonny explained, his words carrying the weight of this lived experience and hard-earned wisdom. "I learned this invaluable lesson from him, though it wasn't one he intended to teach."

He recounted the story of the red minibike languishing in Mr. Buchanan's garage. "Knowing he was not riding it, I asked what he planned to do with it, all the while hoping he'd offer to sell it to me. But sadly, that minibike sat rusting in Mr. Buchanan's garage long after he passed.

"Though indirect, I'm so grateful Mr. Buchanan's actions or lack thereof taught me the importance of letting go of possessions no longer needed and blessing others in the process—one I feel very strongly about and work hard to instill in you," underscoring the subtle yet profound impact of Mr. Buchanan's unintentional teachable moment.

As Roy expressed empathy for his father's missed opportunity, Sonny's smile held a hint of mischief, foreshadowing the unexpected twist in the tale. With a twinkle in his eye, he revealed the serendipitous turn of events that had led to an unforeseen blessing—a testament to the cyclical nature of fate and the boundless potential for redemption.

"Well, Son, there's actually more to the minibike story," Sonny revealed, his eyes twinkling with amusement as he recounted the unexpected turn of events that had led to a fortuitous discovery.

"One day, during one of my neighborhood walks," he continued, "I spotted a blue minibike sitting in a pile of trash on the curbside." Roy's eyes widened with intrigue, his imagination already whirring with the possibilities of such a find.

"I got it out of the trash and pushed it all the way home," Sonny gestured his hands animatedly as if reliving the moment, "and my neighbor offered to fix it. Later that day, I heard what sounded like a minibike racing up and down the street." He paused for dramatic effect, a grin spreading across his face. "I thought it was my friends, but when I ran to the window, I discovered it was Norm speeding up and down the street on the minibike I'd found in the trash.

"One man's trash can truly be another man's treasure," Sonny mused, a hint of wisdom in his voice.

With each word, Sonny's story unfolded like a testament to the transformative power of second chances and the joy of unexpected blessings, leaving Roy marveling at the serendipitous chain of events that had unfolded.

As they resumed their hike, they walked in companionable silence, their hearts lightened by the shared memories and the subtle, yet profound lessons learned along the way. In the gentle embrace of nature, they found solace and wisdom, united in their journey of discovery and growth.

Sporting Tales and Community Bonds

As Sonny and Roy trekked homeward, the forest seemed to exhale a soft sigh of contentment, its ancient whispers echoing tales of generations past. The dense foliage swayed gently in the breeze, casting fleeting shadows that danced along the forest floor, a silent testament to the passage of time.

"Junior high school was a time of discovery and growth," Sonny reminisced, "I immersed myself in sports, finding solace and camaraderie on the field and court."

As they traversed the winding paths, Sonny recounted his affinity for football, a passion that had ignited his spirit and fueled his determination. His memories of neighborhood games and shared laughter filled the air, painting a portrait of youthful exuberance and boundless energy.

Sonny's connection to his Aunt Dee Dee added another layer to the tapestry of his youth, her presence a beacon of strength and inspiration.

With fondness, he recalled her unwavering support and encouragement, her belief in his potential shaped his coming-of-age journey in profound ways.

"Aunt Dee Dee was a guiding light in my life," Sonny reflected, his voice filled with reverence. "She instilled in me a sense of purpose, urging me to strive for greatness in all that I do."

Through Aunt Dee Dee's guidance, Sonny found himself immersed in the fabric of his community, his summer job with Job Corps instilling within him a sense of responsibility and civic duty. Sonny was tasked with walking the neighborhoods and informing people they had rubbish (i.e., abandoned cars, old refrigerators, rusted barrels, etc.) in their yards that had to be removed. He'd then document his observations and submit them to city officials.

Thereafter, residents had a limited amount of time to remove the items from their yards. If they failed to do so, they would receive a follow-up visit from the neighborhood police. This job was a promising start to Sonny becoming a police officer. Walking the neighborhoods, he learned the importance of service and stewardship, which laid the foundation for a future dedicated to making a difference in law enforcement.

The Making of a Good Man

As they continued their walk home, Roy listened intently as his dad shared stories from his early teenage years, particularly highlighting the pivotal role his cousin Jeanie played in shaping his character.

Sonny reminisced about the times he spent with his cousins Craig and Jeanie, who was more like a second mother to him. "Jeanie kept us busy, that's for sure." Sonny chuckled, recalling their frequent trips to the YMCA. "We practically lived there—swimming, playing basketball, and lifting weights."

Roy nodded, intrigued by the vibrant picture his dad painted of their youthful adventures. "Sounds like you guys had a blast," he remarked.

"Absolutely," Sonny replied, his eyes glinting with fond memories.

Amidst their myriad activities, swimming had been a favorite pastime, a sanctuary where Sonny and Craig found comfort in the cool embrace of the water. Yet, amidst the splashing and laughter, there existed a poignant moment that had left an indelible mark on Sonny's heart.

"There was this one kid," Sonny began, his voice softening as he painted a picture of a boy who had stood out amidst the throng of eager swimmers. "He always came out into the pool area with his towel wrapped all the way around his chest."

Roy, though slightly puzzled, recognized the scene unfolding before him—a classic depiction of childhood innocence tinged with the sting of social ridicule.

"All the kids would tease him and laugh," Sonny continued, his tone heavy with empathy, "saying, 'Look at this little girl.'"

But Sonny, ever the empathetic soul, had seen beyond the surface, recognizing the vulnerability that lay beneath the boy's bravado. With a kindness born of understanding, he had approached the boy, extending a hand of friendship amidst the sea of ridicule.

"I asked him why he wore his towel around his chest and not his waist," Sonny recounted, his voice gentle as he recalled the conversation that had unfolded between two young souls navigating the complexities of masculinity and identity.

"The little boy said that's the way his mom and his sisters wear theirs," Sonny continued, his heart moved by the weight of the boy's words.

In that moment, Sonny became more than a friend—he became a teacher, imparting wisdom borne of experience and empathy.

"I explained to him that boys wear their towels around the waist to cover their private body parts," Sonny recounted, his voice steady as he navigated the delicate terrain of gender norms and self-discovery. "Girls wear their towels around the top to cover their private body parts."

"When boys don't have male role models in their lives, they're prone to emulate the behavior of whomever is in their homes," Sonny reflected, his words echoing with the weight of hard-earned wisdom. "This young man did not have a male figure in his life."

Roy had not given much thought to how he wore his towel, but in this moment, he was grateful his Dad had always been his model.

"All young men, no matter their age, need a male role model in their lives," Sonny concluded, his voice ringing with conviction. "To know how to appropriately practice male norms."

"My time with Craig wasn't all fun and games. Jeanie taught us important life lessons along the way."

One such lesson came during a routine shopping trip with Jeanie, where she instilled in the boys the value of responsibility and respect. "Jeanie made sure we knew how to handle ourselves," Sonny explained. "She'd have us pick out our own clothes and make sure we got a good deal. And when it came time to pay, she taught us to be respectful—even when others weren't."

Roy leaned in, captivated by the story. "Was someone disrespectful to you while you were shopping, Dad?" he asked.

Sonny recounted a moment at the checkout counter when the cashier failed to place the money directly into his hand. "Jeanie didn't hesitate to speak up," Sonny recalled. "She showed us that it's okay to stand up for ourselves, but to always do it with dignity and respect."

Roy nodded in understanding, impressed by his great cousin's unwavering resolve. "She sounds fierce."

"She was," Sonny agreed, his voice steeped with admiration. "Jeanie didn't just teach us about respect—she also made sure we were aware of the world around us."

Indeed, Jeanie's influence extended beyond manners and etiquette. "She got us involved in politics, had educational discussions with us in the car, and made sure we knew how to manage our affairs," Sonny explained. "She was raising us to be good, respectful young men, but she also knew the importance of letting us be kids."

As the sun dipped below the horizon, casting a warm glow over the landscape, Sonny and Roy arrived home, their hearts lightened by the memories shared and the bonds forged along the way. Amidst the hustle and bustle of evening preparations, they found solace in the simple joys of family and fellowship, their shared experiences a testament to the enduring power of love and legacy.

As they settled in for the night, Roy's mind buzzed with excitement, the lessons learned from his father swirling like stars in the night sky. With each passing moment, he felt a deeper connection to his roots, a sense of pride in the lineage of strength and resilience that flowed through his veins.

In the quiet stillness of the night, as dreams danced on the edge of consciousness, Roy drifted into slumber, his heart filled with gratitude for the wisdom imparted by his father and the boundless possibilities that lay ahead on their journey of discovery and growth.

Academic Excellence and Teamwork

Sipping his customary cup of morning tea, Sonny reflected on the coming-of-age experiences he'd shared with his son over the weekend. He was rather impressed by the way Roy was fully engaged to the point where he was able to relay the lessons he'd taken away from his lived experiences.

There was so much more he wanted to share—events from his high school, college, and professional experiences that helped shape his character. For a moment, he felt overwhelmed because he'd hoped to convey all of the character-building lessons he'd learned during this three-day weekend.

Sonny wanted to honor his son's request to gain an understanding of what it takes to develop the character traits of a good man. However, he was fearful that if he did not respond while Roy's interest was piqued, he might not have his undivided attention on this topic again. But in that moment, he was comforted by the fact that Roy was a resolute learner—he was the one who asked, and given how engaged he had been, Sonny was confident Roy would stay the course.

Afterall, their father-son duo was a lifetime in the making. Whatever he failed to communicate this weekend, he would be sure to communicate the next. No sooner had he finished this thought did a freshly energized Roy emerge from his room asking, "What are we gonna do today, Dad?"

"Well, son," Sonny answered, "since we were out the last couple of days, I thought we'd stick around the house today. You can help me clean up the backyard, and later we can light the firepit and enjoy some s'mores."

Excited for the day's plan, Roy and Sonny took to the yard to begin working. As they began, Roy reminded his dad that the last thing he'd shared was about his job with Job Corp and the lessons he'd learned from Aunt Dee Dee and cousin Jeanie.

"Were you still in junior high then?" Roy asked.

"No," Sonny clarified, "by that time, I was a sophomore in high school, so I need to backtrack and tell you about my transition from junior high to high school."

As Sonny and Roy worked in the backyard, the crisp southern air carried with it the echoes of Sonny's high school days, a time of transition and growth that had left an indelible mark on his character. With each rake of the leaves and stray branches, Sonny wove a tapestry of memories, sharing glimpses of his academic journey with his attentive son.

"High school was a pivotal time for me," Sonny reflected, his voice filled with reverence for the formative years that had shaped his path. "It was a time of academic rigor and personal discovery, a journey marked by hard work and unwavering determination."

As they cleared away the fallen foliage, Sonny recounted his introduction to the halls of Beecher High School, a beacon of opportunity and potential.

Walking those familiar paths, he had found himself surrounded by a diverse tapestry of peers, each with their own strengths and aspirations.

"High school was a melting pot of talent and ambition," Sonny explained. "There, I quickly learned the importance of surrounding myself with like-minded individuals, forming study groups that would propel me toward academic success."

With each passing day, Sonny found himself immersed in a world of collaboration and camaraderie, his study groups becoming a cornerstone of his educational journey. From late-night study sessions to collaborative projects, he had forged lasting friendships and honed his skills as a critical thinker and problem-solver.

"Working with my peers was instrumental in my success," Sonny continued, his voice filled with pride. "Together, we tackled challenges head-on, leveraging our collective knowledge and expertise to overcome obstacles and achieve our goals."

Absorbing his Dad's words, Roy questioned, "So, did you have any standout study partners?"

Sonny's face lit up with a reminiscent smile. "Oh, absolutely," he replied. "One of my closest study buddies was Karen Shim. Joe and I would sit at her house, and she'd make us study. She knew she was the smartest, but she didn't lord her intelligence over us. Instead, she pushed us to study hard because she wanted to see Joe and me succeed."

Roy chuckled at the thought. "Sounds like she kept you two in line."

"Definitely," Sonny agreed with a laugh. "Our study group for science was Joe, Karen, and me."

Roy leaned in, eager to hear more. "What was it like studying with them?"

Sonny's expression softened with fond memories. "Karen taught us how to study, write out goals, and achieve them."

He paused for a moment, a nostalgic glint in his eyes. "You know, we still remember an answer to a test question from science," he continued. "The answer to number 6 was 'effervescent.' We still laugh about that to this day."

As Roy absorbed this lesson, Sonny persisted, his gaze drifting into the past. "Son, I know you know being a successful student takes hard work and dedication. More specifically, when you get to high school, the key to excelling there is to develop sound study habits. Get with a group of friends that want to study, and you'll be sure to enjoy academic wins together."

Roy nodded, taking in his Dad's advice. "Thanks, Dad," he said sincerely. "I'll keep that in mind."

Sonny then shared one of his fondest memories from high school—a victorious courtroom competition against Powers High School, the reigning debate champs. With Kristin by his side, he had faced the challenge with confidence and determination, emerging triumphant in the face of adversity.

"It was a testament to the power of teamwork and preparation," Sonny exclaimed, his eyes sparkling with pride. "Together, we proved that with dedication and hard work, anything is possible."

As they continued their yard tasks, Roy couldn't help but feel inspired by his father's stories of triumph and resilience. With each lesson learned, he gained a deeper appreciation for the value of education and the importance of surrounding oneself with a supportive community.

Triumph on the Track

Persisting through the arduous task of raking leaves, Sonny continued to weave tales of his high school days, a time filled with challenges, triumphs, and the relentless pursuit of excellence. With each sweep of the rake, memories of his track team days came flooding back, and he eagerly shared his journey with his rapt son.

"Knowing my love for football, you'd think I'd join the football team," Sonny mused, a hint of nostalgia in his voice, "but I decided to try out for the track team instead."

Roy, remembering their conversation from the day before, questioned, "Track? Really?"

"I was in the band. Since band and football occurred at the same time, I had to choose another sport."

Sonny continued, a wistful smile playing on his lips. "Back then, making the track team wasn't about varsity or junior varsity—it was about proving yourself, plain and simple."

As he recounted his days as an 800-meter and mile runner, Sonny's eyes sparkled with the thrill of competition. "I loved the challenge of the mile," he explained. "There were a few other milers on the team, but I always pushed myself to compete with the best—and for me, that person was Bill Clifton."

Roy, recalling his father's competitive spirit from the backflip story, chimed in, "So Bill had you beat on the track, just like Joe with backflips!"

Sonny chuckled, nodding in agreement. "Exactly. This proved I had room to grow, and they pushed me to be my best, on and off the track."

Despite finishing fourth or fifth in his freshman year races, Sonny never lost his competitive edge. "I always gave it my all, especially in that final stretch."

But it wasn't just personal drive that fueled Sonny's success—it was also the pressure from his coach and teammates, particularly the seniors, who demanded nothing but the best from their fellow athletes.

"The seniors on the team were relentless," Sonny recounted, his tone grave. "They held us to a higher standard, pushing us to excel even when it seemed impossible."

Roy listened intently as Sonny shared the story of a particularly intense moment in the locker room—an experience that had solidified his resolve and transformed him into a true competitor.

"That moment changed everything for me," Sonny confessed, his voice carrying the weight of years of reflection. "It made me realize that success wasn't just about individual performance—it was about being part of something greater than myself."

Roy nodded, his gaze fixed on his father as he absorbed the wisdom woven into the fabric of Sonny's tale.

"When faced with insurmountable challenges, remember this mantra," Sonny urged, his voice laced with a blend of solemnity and fervor. "Heat plus concentration equals performance. Performance minus concentration equals heat."

As the words settled over them like a mantle of understanding, Sonny delved deeper into the crucible of competition that had shaped his character and forged his resolve.

"This is how it played out," Sonny continued, his voice steady as he painted a picture of the relentless pursuit of excellence that defined his time on the track team. "Every year, our track team was #1 in the state."

Roy's eyes widened with awe as he imagined the pressure-cooker environment of a team perpetually poised at the pinnacle of success.

"After the track meet one day," Sonny recounted, his voice growing somber, "the seniors followed me into the bathroom where the toilets were filled with feces."

A shudder ran through Roy as he listened, his heart heavy with the weight of his father's past trials.

"They asked me how well I thought I ran," Sonny continued, his tone tinged with sullenness. "I finished in 5th place. That wasn't good enough."

Roy gasped, his mind reeling at the cruelty of his father's teammates.

"Those seniors picked me up and held me upside down over the toilet," Sonny confessed, his voice raw with the memory of humiliation and betrayal.

"Oh no, Dad!" Roy exclaimed, his heart aching with empathy for the boy his father had once been.

"But that moment," Sonny continued, his voice rising with quiet determination, "fueled a fire within me."

From that crucible of adversity emerged a champion—a competitor forged in the fires of trial and tempered by the relentless pursuit of greatness.

"I may not have ever beaten Bill," Sonny reflected, "but the pressure and heat I felt from my highly competitive teammates turned me into a true competitor."

Sonny and his teammates were not merely athletes—they were disciples in the school of hard knocks, under the tutelage of a coach who commanded respect and inspired greatness.

Sonny's coach, Coach Crane, was a legend, his booming voice a clarion call that echoed across the dusty expanse of the track, heard by all who dared to set foot upon its hallowed ground. His words were a mantra, a relentless refrain that spurred his charges to ever greater heights of achievement.

Sonny recounted, "He'd bellow, 'You better go now!' and his voice carried on the wind like a thunderclap."

For Sonny and his teammates, track practice was not merely a grueling regimen—it was a crucible of discipline and determination, where every stride on the uneven dirty track was a testament to their resilience.

As they pounded the earth beneath their feet, sweat pouring down their brows and muscles burning with exertion, they knew that failure was not an option—not when their coach demanded nothing less than excellence.

Running on that unforgiving terrain day in and day out made them not only stronger, but faster than any other team—a force to be reckoned with on the track and a testament to the transformative power of dedication and discipline.

For Sonny and his teammates, Coach Crane was more than just a mentor—he was a visionary, a guiding light whose unwavering faith in their abilities propelled them to heights they never thought possible. Under his watchful eyes, they trained not as mere mortals, but as champions in the making—convinced of their own greatness and determined to prove themselves worthy of the mantle they had been given.

In that moment, a quiet pride was evident in Sonny's demeanor as he spoke. "Son, this is why I train all the track athletes in the surrounding area," he explained, his voice carrying the weight of his conviction. "This is my way of giving back."

Roy nodded, absorbing his father's words. "So, you're like Coach Crane to them," he remarked, connecting the dots.

"Exactly," Sonny affirmed with a smile. "In the way Coach Crane's voice challenged us on the track, my voice serves the same purpose for these young athletes, many of whom became state champions."

Roy looked at his father with sheer admiration. "That's incredible, Dad. Way to pass on Coach Crane's legacy."

Sonny's smile widened, a sense of fulfillment shining in his eyes. "When you master a skill, son, you're responsible for sharing it with others so that they, too, can excel," he declared, his voice filled with conviction. "That's what Coach Crane taught me, and it's a lesson I humbly impart to you."

As they finished stacking the last pile of leaves, Roy couldn't help but feel a sense of awe at his father's resilience and determination. And as they headed inside for a lunch break, he carried with him a newfound appreciation for the power of teamwork and the importance of pushing oneself to new heights. In Sonny's stories, he found inspiration and guidance—a roadmap for his own journey of self-discovery and growth.

A Runner's Escape

Taking a break from their yard work, Sonny and Roy retreated to the back porch to enjoy a brief respite. It was there that Sonny decided to share a harrowing tale from his past—a brush with death that had left an indelible mark on his soul.

"One Saturday morning," Sonny began, his voice tinted with a mixture of tension and nostalgia, "I decided to go for a long jog from my dad's house to my mom's house. It was about a 10-mile distance, but I was determined to do it."

As he recounted the events of that fateful day, Sonny described the rhythmic cadence of his footsteps and the steady beat of his heart as he pushed himself forward. He had no watch to track his pace, relying instead on the mental tempo he'd learned from his track coach.

"But around mile nine," Sonny continued, his expression darkening, "my peaceful run was interrupted by the sudden appearance of a large dog, charging at me with ferocious intent."

Roy gasped, his eyes widening in disbelief at the peril his father had faced. "What did you do?" he asked, his voice trembling with concern.

Sonny's lips curved into a wry smile as he recounted his daring escape. "I jumped onto the roof of a parked car, narrowly evading the dog's snapping jaws. Thankfully, the owner called the dog back, and I was able to continue my run."

But, the danger was far from over. As Sonny neared his mother's house, another threat emerged—this time, in the form of a suspicious car. He could see his uncle Lester's car in his mom's driveway but feared what was about to happen would not give his uncle enough time to get to him.

"I sensed it was going to be a drive-by," Sonny recalled, his voice tense with the memory. "I looked for somewhere to hide, but there was nowhere to go. Just then, the driver jumped out of the car and pointed his gun at my chest.

"In desperation, I yelled out, 'Uncle L!' He came running, and the strange man got back in his car and drove off, declaring, 'Boy, I'm from Detroit! I'll kill you!'"

Roy listened in rapt attention as Sonny described the heart-stopping moment when his uncle's timely intervention had saved him from what very likely could've been his death.

"It was a wake-up call," Sonny admitted, his tone somber. "Living in our neighborhood, you had to be vigilant at all times. Danger could strike at any moment, and you had to be prepared to defend yourself. Sadly, countless young men's lives were prematurely taken by gun violence before their eighteenth birthdays."

Roy nodded in understanding, his young mind grappling with the harsh realities his father had faced growing up. For Sonny, that day had been a stark reminder of the fragility of life—and the importance of quick thinking and resilience in the face of danger.

"As strange as it sounds," Sonny concluded, his gaze distant with reflection, "my decision to go running that day could have cost me my life, but I believe my commitment to the discipline of running may have saved my life. Running taught me to persevere, to think fast, and to act even faster—a lesson that continues to preserve my life to this day."

A Gift on Four Wheels

As they returned to the yard to tackle more scattered leaves, Sonny resumed his storytelling, weaving a tapestry of memories from his youth. "I still remember the day we made the front page of the Flint Journal," he reminisced, his voice tinged with pride.

Beecher Bucs State Champs Again

That headline was like music to their ears, especially since it was their third consecutive win."

Roy listened intently, eager for the tale to unfold. But Sonny's narrative took an unexpected turn as he revealed a surprise gift from his father—a car that had been hiding in plain sight.

"You see, son," Sonny recalled, "my first car sat in the garage for an entire year before I even knew it was there. It was a Cutlass."

Roy's eyes widened in amazement as he imagined the scene of Sonny's birthday revelation. "So, you had no idea you had a car?" he asked incredulously.

"None whatsoever," Sonny admitted with a grin. "The garage was detached from the house, so it was fairly easy for me to be totally oblivious that it was there. And my sisters did most of my chores, so I didn't have any reason to go to the garage. But on my 18th birthday, senior year of high school, my dad handed me a set of keys and told me to check the garage. That's when I discovered my birthday gift—a four-door dark green Cutlass waiting for me, which we affectionately called the Big Green Pickle."

Roy laughed at the nickname for the car, finding humor in the quirky moniker. "The Big Green Pickle," he repeated, shaking his head in amusement.

With newfound freedom on four wheels, Sonny embraced the joys of car ownership, relishing the independence it afforded him. "Having that car changed everything," he explained. "I even quit the track team because, well, who needs to run when you can drive, right?"

Roy nodded in agreement, understanding the allure of automotive freedom. But his curiosity was piqued by Sonny's mention of his sisters' involvement in household chores.

"So, your sisters did most of your chores?" Roy asked, a hint of playful envy in his voice.

Sonny chuckled, reflecting on his childhood indulgences. "Yes, I was quite spoiled by my sisters," he admitted. "Come to think of it, Mom also went above and beyond to make me feel special. She'd cook breakfast every morning, and I'd get whatever I wanted, including freshly squeezed, pulp-free orange juice. It's just what moms do—they have a knack for making their children feel cherished. But if you ask your aunts and uncle, they probably say I was treated especially, special."

Roy smiled, grateful for the love and attention he received from his parents. "Well, you and mom do a pretty good job, too," he replied. "But I wouldn't mind having some sisters to pitch in with my chores."

Laughing, Sonny replied, "I bet you wouldn't!"

There in their yard, this father and son duo bore their souls, their bond strengthened by the shared stories of the past and the promise of adventures yet to come.

Marching to a Different Beat

Resuming their leaf-gathering duties, Roy's curiosity led him to ask his dad about how he spent his newfound free time after leaving the track team.

Senior year brought a shift in Sonny's extracurricular focus, and he found himself drawn more to the vibrant world of the school band. "Well, son," Sonny began, "I didn't have much on my plate senior year, so I decided to dive deeper into the band scene."

Throughout all four years of high school, Sonny had been a part of the band, but it wasn't until his senior year that he truly embraced it. "Band was competitive, let me tell you," Sonny explained with a chuckle. "I played the trombone, but I'll be the first to admit, I wasn't exactly a virtuoso. Still, being with my friends made it all worthwhile."

Roy couldn't help but laugh at the image of his dad struggling with the trombone. "Seriously, Dad? You weren't any good?" he teased.

Sonny nodded, his eyes twinkling with amusement. "Oh, we were terrible," he confessed. "Joe and I were always battling for last place in competitions. We were so bad that they even created a special class just to help us improve."

Despite their lackluster musical abilities, Sonny and Joe found solace in their friendship and the spirited atmosphere of the band. "We may not have been the best musicians," Sonny admitted, "but we gave it our all, especially when it came to marching. That's where we really shined."

The band's competitive spirit drove them to excel, often earning them first place in competitions. "We had some standout performers, like Tracey," Sonny recalled fondly. "She was a trombone expert and always helped us out. But no matter how hard we tried, Joe and I were always at the bottom of the lineup."

Roy chuckled at the thought of his dad's musical misadventures. "Sounds like quite the off-note experience," he cleverly remarked.

"It definitely was," Sonny agreed with a smile. "Our band director was something else, too. He thought he was Michael Jackson, and he put on quite the show at competitions. It was a sight to behold, let me tell you."

The Making of a Good Man

As they continued working, their lighthearted moment of laughter mingled with the rustle of leaves and the distant sounds of the neighborhood. In the rhythm of Sonny's stories, they found a bond that transcended time and circumstance.

Navigating through Adversity to Manhood

Befittingly, as MLK Day unfolded its significance, Sonny took a moment to honor the late Dr. Martin Luther King Jr. Roy, ever the astute observer, noted the synchronicity of Sonny's birth year with Dr. King's tragic assassination, asking, "Dad, did you know you were born the same year Dr. King was assassinated?"

Sonny paused, the connection stirring within him. "I guess I knew that," he responded, his voice laced with introspection, "but I don't think I truly took the time to make that connection. That's incredibly insightful of you, Son!"

In the ensuing quiet, Sonny's mind drifted to Dr. King's message of nonviolent action against inequality. He felt a responsibility to impart this wisdom to Roy, to ensure he understood the struggles and triumphs of past and present black leaders.

"Son," Sonny began, his tone somber, "there were a lot more acts of blatant racism when I was growing up. But given the recent publicized horrific acts of police brutality, sadly, Roy, you've seen just how ugly racism still is."

Navigating through life as a Black man, Sonny knew the importance of preparation. His parents had instilled in him a sense of vigilance, a readiness to face any adversity head-on.

Roy nodded in understanding, recalling the discussions they had during the COVID pandemic. "Dad," he said, "this reminds me of **the talk** we had about staying safe."

"Exactly," Sonny affirmed. "We didn't call it **the talk** then, but my friends and I learned we were susceptible to being mistreated by the cops because of the color of our skin. So, our parents made sure we followed a scripted set of rules should we ever have an encounter with the police. It was about survival, about knowing how to navigate a world that wasn't always fair."

Reflecting on his own upbringing, Sonny couldn't help but think of the rules and boundaries his parents had set for him. "You see, Roy," he explained, "I didn't know it then, but I grew to learn that for my parents, it wasn't just about enforcing curfews or restrictions. It was about teaching me to make wise decisions, to understand the consequences of my actions."

Roy listened intently, realizing the importance of accountability and responsibility. He understood now why his parents had been so strict, why he had been taught to always plan ahead and anticipate potential dangers.

As they finished tidying up the yard, Roy couldn't help but admire his father's resilience and strength of character. "Dad," he said, "I'm glad you chose to listen to your parents. It seems like your life depended on it."

Sonny's face broke into a smile, as a wave of humility washed over him. "I had to," he said simply. "It was the only way to survive, to thrive in a world that often seemed stacked against us.

"When I was young," Sonny continued, "I made a promise to myself. I wasn't going to smoke, do drugs, get my ear pierced, nor get a tattoo. And to this day, I've never done any of those things."

It was a simple declaration, but it spoke volumes about Sonny's unwavering commitment to his principles. He had chosen the path less traveled, the path of integrity and self-discipline.

"These are the things that help a young man become a good man," Sonny explained, his voice steady and sure. "Be true to yourself and others,

The Making of a Good Man

hold fast to your word—even when it's not the popular choice. That's what builds character, Roy."

Unwavering respect blossomed within Roy for his father.

"If you say it, you can do it," Sonny concluded, his words a quiet reminder of the power of determination and conviction. And as they finished their task, Roy knew that he would carry his father's words with him always.

Amidst the bagged leaves and the echoes of history, Sonny knew that he had passed on more than just rules and regulations to his son. He had imparted a legacy of strength, resilience, and unwavering integrity—a legacy that would endure for generations to come.

Beecher High: A Blast from the Past

As they set their attention on the last outdoor task of the day—prepping the firepit for an evening of s'mores—Sonny redirected his conversation, eager to reminisce about the lighter moments of his high school days.

"Now, I know I've shared some pretty heavy topics with you today, Roy," Sonny began, a hint of excitement in his voice, "but in the same breath, I want you to know, high school was lit!"

Roy couldn't help but chuckle at his dad's attempt to bring back outdated slang. "Really, Dad?! No one says lit anymore!"

"Well, I'm bringing lit back!" Sonny retorted playfully. "And while I'm at it, I'm bringing back off the chain, too, because my high school was off the chain!"

Smirking, Roy listened to Sonny boast about Beecher High's dominance in academics, athletics, and extracurriculars.

"Beecher High was on point in every aspect," Sonny declared proudly, his nostalgia evident.

"We were number one in the state for track four years in a row, and we excelled in football, basketball, band, and even mock trial competitions."

As he reminisced, Sonny's eyes sparkled with excitement; he recalled the energetic pep rallies that united the entire school community. "Teddy, our school mascot, was a beast," Sonny exclaimed, his enthusiasm contagious. "He would come out on the floor and do backflip after backflip, getting the crowd hyped, and the crowd would chant 'B-double E-C-H-E-R, Beecher!'"

Roy could feel his dad's enthusiasm as he recounted the electrifying atmosphere of Beecher High's pep rallies and sporting events, where students, parents, teachers, and the band came together to show their unwavering support.

"The events that the student body president and his team would put on during those pep rallies were epic," Sonny reminisced. "Remember I told you our students were about achievement?" Roy nodded eagerly, anxious to hear more. "Well, during our pep rallies, one of the most anticipated events was the announcement of the winners of our senior superlatives competition. The categories included Best Legs—Tamika Lewis, one of our top female athletes, won for the women, and Terence Strong won for the men."

Roy's eyes widened with interest as Sonny listed off the names of his former classmates, each one seemingly more impressive than the last.

"Most Likely to Succeed was Troy Reeves, and the valedictorian Melvin Hornsby, with another top academic, Rebecca Dye were named Top of the Class." Sonny's tone brimmed with admiration. "We also had Prettiest Male and Female. I think it was Mark and, of course, Yalonda Briggs, who won this category.

"Most Athletic was Roy Marble," Sonny continued, casting a fond glance at his son. "He was probably the first person I saw dunk from the free-throw line in real life. Twanny Wilson and Tamika Lewis were the top athletes for the females."

"Oh, and Best Singer was Major Sublett," Sonny concluded with a smile. "We had some superstars in high school. So, your dad was not a stand out; I was just trying to compete with the best, most beautiful, and smartest people I knew. We'd say, 'It must be the Beecher water,' because all of us in our own right possessed exceptional talent."

As Sonny's words echoed in the air, Roy couldn't help but feel a surge of admiration for his Dad and the remarkable classmates who had shared in those unforgettable high school experiences.

In addition to the academics, sports, and superlative competitions, Sonny would be remiss if he neglected to highlight Beecher High's talent shows. During these shows, students showcased diverse talents, from singers to breakdancers. However, though he longed to be on stage, Sonny did not participate in the performance arts.

"Dad, with your love for dancing now, I'm surprised you didn't try out for the talent show back then," Roy remarked curiously.

Sonny chuckled, reflecting on his past hesitations. "I guess I didn't think I had the dancing skills back then, but looking back, maybe I just didn't apply myself."

As the evening sun cast a warm glow over their backyard, father and son continued their soulful exchange, as Sonny bridged the generational gap with shared memories of his high school glory days at Beecher High.

Summer Days and College Dreams

As the evening settled in, Roy, Sonny, and Marsha gathered around the crackling fire pit, ready to indulge in the nostalgic sweetness of s'mores. The warm glow of the flames cast flickering shadows on their faces, reminiscent of evenings spent around a campfire. With the aroma of melting chocolate and toasted marshmallows wafting through the air, Roy's curiosity sparked a conversation about his dad's high school summers.

Sonny regaled Roy with stories of carefree days spent with family, particularly his cousins Stacey, Craig, and Cory. Together, they embarked on adventures filled with moped rides, bike excursions, and snowmobile adventures during winter. The highlight of their summers was visiting a small lake house up north, where they indulged in early morning lake baths and explored the wilderness with the freedom only youth could afford.

The Making of a Good Man

Stacey, the oldest cousin, assumed the role of leader, overseeing their activities and handling most of the cooking. The boys reveled in their freedom, engaging in BB gun battles, fishing expeditions, and spirited banter that shaped Sonny's affinity for good-natured trash-talking.

"We just knew how to have a good time," Sonny said, a twinkle in his eye. "Whether it was biking through town or having BB gun battles in the backyard, we always kept things interesting."

Roy's eyebrows shot up in surprise. "BB gun battles? That sounds intense!"

"It was all in good fun," Sonny reassured, a grin spreading across his face. "But we definitely knew how to talk some trash."

"I still can't believe you trash talked!" Roy exclaimed, turning to Marsha for confirmation.

Marsha nodded, a fond smile playing at her lips. "Oh yes, your dad has a knack for playful banter, especially when he's with his frat brothers."

Sonny shrugged sheepishly. "What can I say? It's all part of my charm."

Roy, amused by his dad's trash-talking past, sought confirmation from Marsha, who affirmed Sonny's penchant for playful banter with his frat brothers. Reflecting on his past, Sonny acknowledged that while he wouldn't encourage Roy to adopt the habit, it had become ingrained in his vocabulary.

Transitioning the conversation, Sonny shared memories of his high school years, highlighting the rigorous preparation for college. Despite facing challenging classes and the daunting SAT exam, Sonny remained focused on his goal of attending Central State University. With unwavering determination, he applied only to his dream school, refusing to entertain the notion of a backup plan.

As Roy questioned the wisdom of not having a backup plan, Sonny defended his single-minded determination, asserting that having a plan B implied a lack of faith in oneself. Their dialogue touched on the difference between planning for life goals versus daily goals, acknowledging that while a plan B may be prudent in some instances, unwavering belief in one's abilities is paramount.

"It's about having faith in your abilities and trusting that you'll make it happen," Sonny explained, his voice firm with conviction. "And when that acceptance letter came, it was the culmination of all those years of hard work paying off."

Roy listened, his admiration for his dad growing with each word. "I can't imagine what that must have felt like," he mused, a sense of awe coloring his tone.

"It was a moment I'll never forget," Sonny admitted, a hint of wistfulness creeping into his voice. "But it also marked the end of an era—the end of those carefree summers with my cousins and friends." The impending departure of his cousins and friends underscored the bittersweet nature of their final summer together before venturing into adulthood.

Their last summer was spent in the familiar embrace of Granny's house, with evenings filled with laughter and camaraderie. Nights in downtown Flint, cruising Saginaw Street in Sonny's cherished Chevy Chevette, provided the backdrop for their final hurrah before parting ways.

As the fire dwindled to embers and the night grew late, Sonny suggested pausing their trip down memory lane. Roy, eager for more stories, expressed his desire to hear every detail of his dad's college days. Promising to share the highlights that shaped him into the man he was now, Sonny led the way inside, leaving the embers of the firepit to glow softly in the darkness, a silent witness to the bonds of family and the passage of time.

PHASE THREE

Journey to Adulthood: From Beecher to College

Eager to share his transition from high school to college and the rites of passage that marked his journey into adulthood, Sonny decided to take Roy on a memorable trip to one of their all-time favorite places. As Saturday morning dawned, they gassed up the RV and headed south to Santee State Park, ready for a weekend of camping beneath the stars.

"Dad, was Poppa White's RV like ours?" Roy inquired, recalling his dad's fond memories of camping in his grandfather's RV.

"Ours is much nicer, but back then, I thought Poppa White's RV was a state-of-the-art model! No one else in our neighborhood owned an RV. I was incredibly fortunate to have had exposure to camping in style growing up, and I wanted to build similar memories with you," Sonny explained, a nostalgic gleam in his eye.

"Speaking of fond memories of trips," Sonny's voice trailed off, "My first drive down to Central

State University as a freshman was one for the books."

Sterling and Sonny, cousins off to college together, were brimming with excitement. Sonny meticulously packed his car the night before, eager to embark on this new chapter of his life. Arriving at Sterl's house at 5 a.m., Sonny found himself waiting anxiously as Sterl and his parents prepared for the journey ahead.

Setting off on the road, Sonny led the way with Sterl following closely behind in his truck. However, their journey took an unexpected turn when, just 30 minutes from their destination, Sonny's car experienced a dramatic explosion, leaving him stranded on the highway. With no cell phones to rely on, Sterl's timely presence saved the day, allowing Sonny to transfer his belongings into his cousin's truck and continue their journey.

"Thankfully, I had a plan," Sonny recalled.

"That's crazy, Dad! How could you possibly have planned for that?" Roy asked.

"I had no way of knowing that would happen, but planning to drive with Sterl saved me from being stranded that day," Sonny replied, acknowledging the importance of having a support system in unforeseen circumstances.

Arriving at Central State University, Sonny found himself engulfed in a whirlwind of paperwork and long lines for class registration, housing, financial aid, and work-study. Despite the chaos, he was determined to navigate this new environment with patience and resilience.

Assigned to the athletes' dorm with Sterl as his roommate, Sonny embraced the camaraderie and excitement of freshman life. However, he soon discovered the upperclassmen's affinity for pranks, falling victim to the infamous "TBA" class that led unsuspecting freshmen on a wild goose chase.

"TBA?" Roy questioned. "One of the locations on my class schedule was labeled 'TBA,' they led us to believe it was a road off Brush Row Road, but 'TBA' actually meant to be announced." Sonny explained.

As Sonny reminisced about his college days spent with cousins who felt more like siblings, he imparted valuable wisdom to Roy, emphasizing the importance of choosing a path that aligns with his aspirations. Reflecting on his decision to pursue a career in law enforcement, Sonny underscored the significance of making meaningful contributions to society, even if it meant foregoing financial wealth.

"Son," Sonny expounded, "college isn't for everyone. What's important is setting career goals. As Granny shared, I always knew I wanted to be a police officer, so college was a necessary stop on my path to protecting and serving my community. However, every profession does not require a college degree."

Roy listened intently, absorbing his dad's words of wisdom and pondering his own journey into adulthood, knowing that whatever path he chose, his dad would be there to guide him every step of the way.

Lessons Learned by the Lake: From Fishing to Freshman Year

When they arrived at Santee State Park, Sonny secured a prime spot facing the serene lake, the perfect backdrop for a weekend escape. As they took in the tranquil beauty of the water, Roy said longingly, "I wish the water was warm enough to go swimming." Sonny nodded in agreement, his mind already drifting toward the possibility of catching dinner with some freshly caught largemouth bass or bluegill.

Determined to make the most of the daylight hours, they hastily gathered their fishing gear, camp chairs, and snack packs, ready to embark on their lakeside adventure.

"Did you have good grades in college, Dad?" Roy inquired as they settled by the water's edge.

"Well son, my GPA was off to a pretty rocky start," Sonny explained.

Roy, needing clarification, interrupted, "What's GPA?"

"GPA stands for grade point average," Sonny explained patiently. "While it isn't emphasized in elementary school, it becomes crucial in high school as you aim for college admission."

Sonny went on to recount his freshman year struggles at Central State University, where he received a disappointing 2.4 GPA in his first quarter. However, rather than letting this setback deter him, it served as a wake-up call, motivating him to study harder and aim higher. From that point on, Sonny made the Dean's list every quarter, with his GPA soaring to an impressive 4.0.

"College is a time for learning and growth," Sonny emphasized. "In addition to academics, it's about developing friendships, honing your skills, and preparing for the real world.

"My alma mater, Central State University in particular, was all about excellence," Sonny mused, his voice filled with excitement. "It's a HBCU [Historically Black College/University], steeped in history, pride, and distinction."

"The Central State University," Sonny repeated, testing the name on his tongue, "was an esteemed community. We were known as Centralians, and we all shared this unwavering commitment to excellence."

Roy, feeling a sense of admiration for the place his dad spoke so fondly of, expressed, "Sounds like Central State University was the place to be."

"It was," Sonny agreed enthusiastically. "The camaraderie among students was incredible. We supported each other, pushed each other to do our best, and shared our knowledge and resources. It was more than just a school—it was like a family. We shared an unbreakable bond that forms when you're surrounded by people who share your goals and aspirations."

Sonny's eyes sparkled as he recalled the influence of Dr. Art Thomas, the university president. "Dr. Thomas always emphasized the importance of spending time in the library. It wasn't just a place to study; it was a sanctuary where we could expand our minds, day and night."

"As I started hanging out with the study crowd," Sonny continued, "I developed more insight and learned how to use my resources effectively. That's the beauty of Central State; it's not just about academics; it's about personal growth." He paused, in reminiscence, adding. "Central State students are like family. I know it sounds cliché, but it's true. We formed unbreakable bonds and could tangibly feel the familial love we shared."

Sonny's tone shifted, becoming more contemplative. "So, son, when you go to school, I hope I can convince you to attend Central. This year, I'm taking you to homecoming. Your uncle EB is bringing your cousins Logan and Dylan, and De Lo will have D2 with him. And we both know how much you admire D2's swag." Roy smiled in agreement.

Sonny could already envision the pending homecoming scene. "Donovan, Dylan, Chase—they'll all be there. And maybe I'll even talk your Auntie Venus into letting Zyon come along. Hanging around these young men will teach you about business, brotherhood, and success."

Concluding, Sonny reached out, placing a hand on his son's shoulder. "Remember, Roy, your education isn't just about what you learn in the classroom—it's also about the people you meet and the experiences you share. My experience at Central State University gave me more than a degree; it gave me a lifetime of memories and relationships."

As Sonny spoke, Roy felt excited about the prospect of attending such a vibrant and supportive institution. "I hope I can go there, too," he said eagerly.

Sonny's eyes lit up with enthusiasm at the thought of his son attending his beloved alma mater. "I hope so too, son—I hope so, too."

Sonny then shared valuable advice on setting goals, stressing the importance of accountability and planning. "Son, practice writing down your goals, set deadlines, and break them down into actionable steps," he advised. "Hold yourself accountable and stay focused on your objectives."

Reflecting on his college experience, Sonny highlighted the significance of being well-rounded and proactive. "College offers opportunities for personal and intellectual enrichment," he explained. "I know you've got quite some time before you need to seriously think about attending college, but when you do, take advantage of extracurricular activities, attend campus events, and immerse yourself in diverse experiences."

Fondly recalling Central State's iconic May weekend and Convocation events, Sonny urged Roy to seize every opportunity to create lasting memories and broaden his horizons.

"As I've said, son, college isn't for everyone," Sonny reiterated. "But for those who choose to pursue it, it's essential to stay committed and adaptable. Don't just follow a prescribed path. Explore different fields, challenge yourself, and strive for excellence in all aspects of life."

As the sun danced across the tranquil lake, Sonny and Roy continued to fish, their conversation drifting between tales of Sonny's college triumphs and the invaluable lessons learned along the way.

Crossing the Burning Sands: A Journey into Greek Life

Beaming with utter nostalgia, Sonny recounted his introduction to Greek life at Central State University.

"Central State was the place where I made friends that I sustained friendships with for over 35 years," he reminisced, reflecting on the enduring bonds forged within the university's vibrant Greek community. "The gatherings in the breezeway after class, watching the Greeks put on shows was better than any movie you've seen."

Roy, intrigued by this glimpse into his father's past, sought clarification. "The Greeks?" he queried.

"Greeks is the collective term used for the brothers of a fraternity and sisters of a sorority."

"Why Greeks?"

"The founders thought the Greek name would only be recognized by students who were intellectually equipped to recognize the language," Sonny explained. "But more than the

The Making of a Good Man

exclusive society, I was drawn to the brotherhood Greek life had to offer."

Sonny then recounted his journey into Greek life, where he ultimately pledged Kappa Alpha Psi, a decision influenced by the fraternity's commitment to excellent achievement and community service.

"When sophomore year came around, I felt it was time to start showing the men of Kappa that I was interested," he continued. "I had to write a letter and also interview with the men of Kappa Alpha Psi. On September 28, 1988, the men of Kappa Alpha Psi hosted their first interest meeting—this was the day pledging started. There were approximately 40 of us there; I remember looking around the room wondering who would make the line with me."

"So, the line is the others pledging with you?" Roy asked. Nodding, Sonny confirmed. Roy, still intrigued by the pledging process, asked, "What did you have to do to pledge?"

The memory of pick-up night was etched into Sonny's mind like a vibrant mural, each detail clear and sharp even after all these years. He leaned back in his chair, his voice carrying the weight of nostalgia as he recounted the excitement of that pivotal evening to his son.

"Picture this, Roy," Sonny began, his tone tinged with excitement. "I was sitting in my dark room, surrounded by silence, waiting for the moment that would determine my fate. Every breath felt heavy with anticipation, every heartbeat echoing in the stillness."

Roy, hanging on his father's every word, asked impatiently "What happened next?"

"Then, suddenly, I heard it," Sonny narrated. "The booming voices of the men of Kappa, singing their signature chant outside my dorm room door. 'Someone's trying to sneak in my frat; Ain't gonna be no stuff like that.' It was figuratively and literally music to my ears."

As he spoke, Sonny's eyes sparkled with the memory of that moment. "And just like that, my door was flung open, and I was snatched out of my room and thrown into a line with the brothers I'd be pledging with. It was a feeling of relief and joy unlike anything I'd ever experienced before, but that was just the beginning. Once we were out in public, the real challenge began."

Sonny went on to describe the rigorous routine of pledging—running to every class, greeting big brothers with elaborate salutations, and studying diligently under the watchful eyes of their mentors. "We had to know everything about

Kappa, inside and out," Sonny explained, his words capturing his line brothers' dedication and camaraderie. "And we did it all together, as a team."

Roy listened raptly, captivated by his father's account of the incredible bond he forged with his line brothers.

"Pledging with my line was an experience like no other," he began, his voice carrying the weight of cherished memories. "We were a group of eleven determined young men, united by our shared goal of becoming Kappas. It took us two years to go through the whole pledging process," he recounted, a hint of amusement in his voice.

Roy's eyebrows shot up in surprise. "Two years? That's a long time, Dad."

Sonny nodded. "Yes, it was quite unusual because the average pledge process lasts four months," he admitted. "But back then, the pledging process was restricted due to concerns about hazing, so it took longer for us to complete. But, son, it was worth it. La Renaissance was and still is one of the best lines at Central State."

"What made your line stand out?" Roy asked, genuinely intrigued.

Sonny's eyes sparkled as he recalled the dedication and camaraderie of his pledge brothers. "What made us the best was the commitment of the brothers who came before us," he explained. "They invested their time and knowledge into our pledge process, ensuring that we were prepared to uphold the values of Kappa and stand together as a brotherhood."

Fascinated by the sense of unity and purpose within his dad's fraternity, Roy prompted, "Tell me about your line brothers?

Sonny grinned, his pride evident as he described each member of his line—one through eleven klub (denoting their line order determined by their height, followed by klub).

"Let me tell you about our one klub," Sonny began, his eyes alight with admiration. "He was the backbone of our line, always there to support us and keep us grounded. His dedication and strength set the tone for our entire pledge process."

"Two klub," Sonny continued, a grin spreading across his face, "was the showstopper. He had moves like nobody else and could dance circles around anyone. Whenever we needed a burst of energy, he was our go-to guy."

"Three klub," Sonny mused, "was the charmer. He had a way with words that could charm the socks off anyone. The ladies couldn't resist him, and he knew how to work that to our advantage."

"Four klub..." Sonny laughed as he remembered their dramatic line brother. "He brought flair and excitement to everything he did. Whether it was reciting information or performing tasks, he did it with gusto and enthusiasm."

"Six klub was our resident model. He was in impeccable shape, always looking like he stepped out of a magazine. His dedication to fitness inspired us all to push ourselves harder.

"Seven klub was our thinker. He was always one step ahead, thinking about the bigger picture and keeping us focused on our goals. Without him, we would have been lost."

"Eight klub," Sonny chuckled, "was the troublemaker. He had a knack for getting us into mischief with his infectious laughter. But despite his antics, he brought a sense of joy and camaraderie to our pledge experience.

"Nine klub was our encyclopedia. He knew everything there was to know about Kappa, always ready with the answers. His knowledge and expertise earned him the respect of the entire line.

"Ten klub was our rock. He was tough as nails, never backing down from a challenge. His strength and resilience inspired us all to keep pushing forward, no matter what.

"And finally, eleven klub was our smooth operator. He had a calm and collected demeanor that kept us grounded, even in the most stressful situations. He was the epitome of cool under pressure."

As Sonny finished recounting each klub, Roy couldn't help but feel a sense of awe. "Wow, Dad," he exclaimed, "sounds like you had an incredible group of guys by your side during pledging. But what about five klub?" he queried, eager to learn more about his dad's role in the brotherhood.

Sonny's eyes twinkled with amusement when Roy realized his omission. "That would be me," he admitted with a grin. "I made sure to know all the information inside and out, just like nine klub, who was our top dog."

Roy, impressed by his father's dedication and intelligence, concluded, "You were the brains of the operation, huh, Dad?"

Laughing, Sonny confirmed, "I knew my stuff, just like I know you're ready to see some footage," he replied, clapping Roy on the shoulder. "When we get home, I'll dust off the VCR in the garage and show you our pledge video so you can see your dad in action."

On the fateful night of February 23, 1990, they stood resolute and triumphant—La Renaissance successfully crossed the burning sands, emerging as tried and true men of Kappa Alpha Psi.

The brotherhood among Sonny's SanDZ remains unwavering, a testament to their commitment to each other and the values of Kappa Alpha Psi. Their line name, symbolic of a new beginning, reflects their dedication to preserving old-school traditions while adapting to modern rules. Despite the challenges they faced in navigating changing regulations, they stayed true to the traditional pledge process, earning admiration as one of the finest Kappa lines at Central State University.

Their bond transcended time and distance, as evidenced by their sustained commitment to attending every homecoming, annual trip, and regular gathering. From renting luxurious mansions in Miami to embarking on unforgettable cruises, their adventures served as opportunities to strengthen their connections and create lasting memories. Recently, their journey took them to Detroit, where four klub, De

Lo, and seven klub, Dirshawn, hosted an unforgettable gathering that left a lasting impression on everyone.

Beyond the fun and camaraderie, their brotherhood was grounded in mutual support and accountability. Monthly Zoom calls kept them connected, while shared prayers reinforce their spiritual bond. They not only celebrate each other's successes, but also provide unwavering support during life's challenges. Whether it's discussing real-life situations or ensuring each member's physical and mental well-being through regular check-ups, they prioritize each other's welfare.

Their commitment to excellence extends beyond their brotherhood, as evidenced by their collective success as Kappa men. Each member of their line has achieved success in their respective fields, serving as role models for future generations. Their families view them with admiration, recognizing their kindness, generosity, and dedication to uplifting others.

As Sonny shared his pledging experience with Roy, he hoped he'd instilled in him the importance of emulating the integrity, compassion, and excellence his SanDZ embodied.

The Making of a Good Man

Admiring his dad's tenacity, while recognizing the lengths his dad took to pledge, Roy asked, "Was there anyone who didn't cross the burning sands with you when you pledged?"

Sonny reflected on four individuals who had stood out during that time, four young men who, despite their efforts, did not make it through the process. Eric Byrd (EB), James Evans, Ant Jackson, and Charles Byrd were all smart, dedicated individuals who applied themselves fully, but fate had different plans for their journey with La Renaissance. Despite not joining the line initially, they continued their quest and eventually pledged with another group of brothers. However, to this day, they were respected for their efforts by La Renaissance who acknowledge their perseverance in crossing the burning sands. Each of them went on to achieve success in their respective fields: Eric excelled as a vice president and senior executive in banking, James became a licensed attorney, Ant dedicated himself to improving young men's lives as a State Farm agent and educator in the Detroit school system, and Charles is a manufacturing engineer. Their bond and brotherhood served as a testament to their enduring friendship and shared experiences.

"The key to success is never quitting," Sonny emphasized. "Even if you don't achieve your goals right away, perseverance is essential."

As Roy listened, he gained a genuine appreciation for the resilience and brotherhood that defined his father's Greek experience.

Brotherhood beyond Bloodlines

With no fish hooked and the noonday sun blazing, they propped the fishing poles up to eat their snack packs.

Roy tilted his face toward his father. Curious about the fraternity bond between his dad and Uncle Spencer, he asked, "So my Uncle Spencer is your line brother?"

Sonny grinned, nodding in affirmation. "You got it! I also call him my SanDZ, which signifies we crossed the burning sands together."

Roy's eyes widened with excitement. "So, I have 11 uncles?!"

"You actually have 12! You have your uncle Damien, my 10 SanDZ, and your uncle EB," Sonny confirmed.

"One klub, Dr. Steven Rathers Jr., is the pastor of All Believers Bible Church and school principal," Sonny began, launching into a rundown of his fraternity brothers' accomplishments. "Two Klub, kweisi gharreau, is a brand strategist, poet, and activist. Three Klub,

Spencer Ashford, is retired from the military where he served as US Army LTC. Now he works as a project coordinator and medical simulations. Four klub, DeAngelo Alexander, is the superintendent of the Service Learning District and president of Elite School Operations."

Roy's attention was caught as Sonny recapped his own achievements. "As you know, I'm five klub," Sonny noted, "retired law enforcement criminologist." In this moment, Roy recalled Granny's stories of Sonny's childhood declaration, reconciling his dad's aspirations became his reality.

Eager to prove he knew his dad's professional accomplishments, Roy added, "You're also the inventor of the Double R Strong Bar!"

Smiling, Sonny acknowledged Roy's recognition of his invention. "That's right, son," he affirmed, his eyes lighting up with enthusiasm. "The Double R Strong Bar is indeed a revolutionary piece of workout equipment, and it's been embraced by many top high schools and professional athletes."

Reflecting on the genesis of the Double R Strong Bar, Sonny's voice softened with gratitude. "God gave me this wonderful idea to invent the Double R Strong Bar. Even if no one else ever used it, knowing that it came from divine inspiration makes it a masterpiece in my eyes."

Sonny's pride swelled as he recalled the first endorsement of his invention. "Michael Scurlock from the Carolina Panthers was the first to endorse the Double R Strong Bar. And since then, it's been embraced by major athletes at the professional level, all the way down to high schools. And you know what, son? They've found great success with it."

Roy, absorbing every detail of his father's achievement, understood the Double R Strong Bar wasn't just a piece of equipment—it was a testament to his dad's ingenuity and determination to make a positive impact in the world of sports.

Returning to sharing his SanDZ's accomplishments, Sonny proceeded, "Six klub, Ian Bullock, is an engineer and the senior director of Operational Excellence. Seven klub, Dirshawn King, is the president and CEO of Pinnacle Security Solution, LLC and DHS assistant federal security director of law enforcement. Eight klub, Daryl Massie, is an educator, coach, and athletic director. Nine klub, Dr. Eric High, is a renowned gastroenterologist. Ten klub, Dr. Vernon Myers, retired from the military as a United States Army colonel, deputy executive director, US Army Contracting Command-Orlando, and eleven klub, Anthony Robinson, is an artist and art educator."

Reflecting on the challenges they faced during their pledging process, Sonny remarked, "We started with approximately 40 interested individuals, but left as one unit: La Renaissance 11–men of Kappa Alpha Psi."

Sonny recounted the fraternity's commitment to community service and their belief in achieving greatness. "One underlining lesson I want you to take away from our pledging experience," Sonny said earnestly to Roy, "is that you can achieve anything. Believe in yourself, take action, and never doubt your ability to succeed."

Pondering his dad's crystalized point, Roy felt inspired by the legacy of achievement within Kappa Alpha Psi, knowing that with determination and belief, greatness was within reach.

College Adventures: Stepping Up to Challenges

When they finished their lunch, they returned to their fishing poles. Roy noticed his bait was gone, but he had no fish in hand. Sonny suggested they reposition themselves to a different part of the lake.

Once settled into a new spot, Sonny continued talking about college. "Some of the most exciting, carefree times in my life were in college." Nostalgia laced his voice.

His SanDZ truly gave him the courage to step out of his comfort zone.

"The things I didn't achieve while I was in high school, I wanted to achieve in college," Sonny explained, recalling his ambitious college bucket list. "One thing on my list was to be in a talent show. So many others had similar aspirations. I still remember this guy who just knew he was Ralph Tresvant from the group New Edition. He had his looks and his dance moves."

"Who's New Edition?" Roy asked.

Sonny chuckled. "Oh, my goodness, son—who's New Edition?! One of the best male R&B groups of all time!" Whipping out his phone, Sonny scrolled to Amazon Music, selected one of the group's most popular songs, and attempted to sing along: "If it isn't love, why do I feel this way? Why does she stay on my mind?"

Roy, wincing at the sound of his dad's off-tone pitch, pleaded, "Dad, I think you should let them sing it. You're scaring away the fish."

Hilariously undeterred, Sonny continued his story, reminiscing about forming a group with his friends to participate in a talent show, despite lacking vocal talent.

"The day of the talent show we decided to wear soft pink tuxedo style dress shirts with gray jeans and hard sole shoes so we could slide across the stage. When the music started, and the lights hit the stage, the crowd went wild!" Sonny recounted. "And when the announcer read the name of the winners, the crowd lost their minds when we were named the first-place winners."

"So, you won without actually singing?" Roy questioned.

"It was more about our dance moves and stage performance," Sonny explained with a grin.

Once the talent show victory was behind him, Sonny set his sights on another challenge: becoming Homecoming King.

"What did you have to do to compete?" Roy inquired.

Sonny relished sharing the story with his son. "It was intense! We had to do everything from giving speeches to showing off our talents. Rallying support from the students was no joke!"

"Sounds like a lot of pressure."

"You have no idea," Sonny simpered. "But it was worth it. I wanted that crown more than anything."

As the day of the Homecoming King announcement arrived, nerves crackled in the air. Sonny and Solomon stood side by side, both knowing they were the frontrunners.

"We're still counting," someone from Solomon's camp would say, followed by reassurances from Sonny's supporters that he was in the lead.

The tension stretched on, each moment feeling like an eternity. But amidst the nerves, there was a mutual respect between Sonny and Solomon that couldn't be ignored.

Though they were in competition, they did the talent portion of the competition together.

They surprised everyone with a karate skit; as they performed the fight scene, someone backstage did the voiceover. The crowd erupted in laughter and applause as they executed their routine flawlessly, their friendship shining through even in competition.

"We were rivals on stage," Sonny recalled, "but offstage, we were brothers."

As Sonny recounted the tense vote count, Roy hung on to every word, eager to hear the outcome.

"When THE moment arrived, the announcer read, 'Our new Homecoming King is Sonny!' and the crowd erupted in cheer, chanting 'Sonny! Sonny! Sonny!'" Sonny recalled with humility.

"That must have been everything!" Roy remarked.

"It was a great feeling," Sonny agreed.

Despite the nail-biting wait and the fierce competition, Sonny and Solomon's friendship endured. They continued to support each other, celebrating victories and milestones together.

Years later, Sonny still looked up to Solomon with admiration. "He's a true king," Sonny said with a smile, "not just because of a title, but because of how he lives his life and treats others."

Shifting the conversation to step shows, late-night study sessions, fraternity gatherings, and cherished friendships, Sonny continued imparting wisdom about striving for success and embracing failure.

Roy absorbed his father's words, grateful for the insight.

"College was all about learning, growing, and making memories that last a lifetime," Sonny concluded, a sense of gratitude evident in his voice.

College and Life Decisions

The cool of the afternoon seemed to draw the fish closer to the banks of the lake. Sonny and Roy, growing slightly restless, worried about not catching dinner before daylight faded. Just then, Sonny's storytelling was interrupted by a sharp tug on his fishing pole.

Excitedly, Roy exclaimed, "I think you got one, Dad!"

Sonny, now standing, engaged in a brief battle of wills with whatever was on the other end of his line. After a few moments, he reeled in their dinner—a 14-inch bass.

Considering whether to wait for another catch, Sonny weighed the dwindling daylight against the need to clean the fish and build a fire. He decided it was best to call it a day.

Using an onsite camp table as a cleaning station, Sonny guided Roy through the process of gutting and scaling the fish, a skill he'd learned from his mom who was an expert at catching, scaling, gutting, and cleaning them.

Meanwhile, he set about building a fire, modern style, using the firepit, wood, lighter fluid, and a match.

As they roasted their freshly caught fish over the crackling fire, Roy beamed with excitement, as if he himself had reeled in the catch.

While watching their dinner cook, Roy returned his thoughts to his father's college days. "Did you join a team in college, Dad?"

Sonny explained how, despite his desire to do it all, he had to prioritize his time and make sacrifices. Instead of joining a team, he worked a work-study job traveling with the girls' volleyball team, driving the college bus, and learning valuable lessons from Coach Turner.

Reflecting on the importance of wise decision-making, Sonny shared insights into managing finances, particularly credit cards, and emphasized the significance of thinking through choices and considering their long-term impact.

"College students are often targeted by credit card companies," Sonny explained, "because they know they're new to managing money and may not fully grasp the implications of using credit wisely. It's so easy to fall into the trap of thinking that credit cards are free money, but they can quickly become a burden if you're not careful."

He went on to explain the importance of understanding interest rates, minimum payments, and the consequences of carrying a balance. Sonny emphasized the significance of thinking through choices and considering their long-term impact, especially when it came to financial decisions.

Roy listened intently, absorbing his father's words of wisdom by the tranquil lakeside, where lessons in fishing and life intertwined.

The Value of Integrity

Roy, filled with excitement at the prospect of finally eating a fish they caught, exclaimed in a playful tone, "I'm gonna tell everyone I caught this one, Dad!"

Sonny chuckled. "You can tell them you did, but let's remember the truth."

Roy nodded.

"But on the topic of telling the truth," Sonny continued, shifting the conversation toward a more serious note, "Son, your word is your integrity. People will believe in you if you do what you say you're going to do. Your actions are important. You want people to trust you, and that is a reflection of your character."

"Character means a lot," he emphasized. "It's about the mental and moral qualities distinctive to an individual. Make sure you build your character every day. Have morals—standards of behavior or beliefs concerning what is and is not acceptable for you to do. Don't just follow the crowd; do what is right."

Sonny shared a personal anecdote from his pledge days, recounting a time when he struggled to maintain his strict study patterns and ended up failing a midterm. Despite the temptation to cheat, he chose to uphold his integrity, knowing that cheating would contradict the values of the fraternity he was striving to represent. Ultimately, his honesty paid off when his professor allowed his final exam to cancel out his midterm.

"Dad, you know I was only kidding," Roy replied, sensing the shift in tone.

"I know, Son," Sonny reassured him, "but as we've been discussing the characteristics of a good man, it's important to reiterate the significance of upholding your integrity in every aspect of your life."

Fireside Feasts and Family Bonds

Under the vibrant night sky, Roy and Sonny nestled by the crackling campfire, preparing their freshly caught fish for dinner. As they savored each bite of their simple yet satisfying meal, their shared love for food was evident—like father, like son.

Reflecting on their family traditions, Sonny shared how meals often became the centerpiece of cherished memories. Whether it was care packages from his oldest sister and Aunt Lovie, or visits from relatives, family support was a constant during his college days. Sonny fondly recalled the day his entire family surprised him during his fraternity celebration, reinforcing the importance of breaking bread together.

Amidst the warmth of the fire, they couldn't resist ending the night with s'mores, a perfect segue into celebrating Sonny's crowning achievement: graduation. With his family proudly watching, Sonny received his degree with honors, a testament to his dedication and balanced approach to life.

To mark the occasion, Sonny's dad gifted him a trip to the Bahamas, with Aunt Lovie ensuring he wasn't alone by arranging for Stacey to accompany him. Their adventures on the island exposed them to authentic Bahamian culture, creating memories they'd treasure forever.

Upon their return, Sonny's mom threw a lively graduation party, uniting his frat brothers and family in celebration. As they danced and reveled in the joy of the moment, it was clear that their bond extended far beyond bloodlines.

As the night drew to a close, Sonny and his dad retreated to the RV, grateful for the shared experiences and the enduring strength of their family ties.

Despite not being able to attend church in person that Sunday, Sonny and Roy felt grateful for the chance to tune in to the morning service online. As they lounged lakeside, bowls of frosted flakes in hand, they immersed themselves in the message of the day via Roy's iPad.

The Making of a Good Man

The sermon challenged them to let God's guidance permeate every aspect of their lives, a message that resonated deeply with Sonny. As he listened to the pastor's words, he couldn't help but reflect on a pivotal moment in his life, one that had affirmed his faith in God's providence.

"I remember when Granny took me to South Carolina after college," Sonny began, a wistful tone coloring his voice. "Though I didn't fully know it then, later it became clear that God's hand was guiding me every step of the way."

As he spoke, memories flooded back—of uncertain times, of moments of clarity, of feeling the undeniable presence of being called to something greater than himself.

The message of the day, centered around Luke Chapter 6:45, echoed Sonny's own experiences. "It's true," he mused. "What's in your heart is reflected in your words and actions."

Smiling as he recalled the trip, Sonny continued, "I had a job lined up, but instead of working at Kmart for the summer, Granny asked me to drive us to South Carolina for a family wedding. When we arrived, I was captivated by the beauty of the place and the warmth of my cousins. I thought to myself: I could live here."

With that thought, Sonny seized the opportunity, sending copies of his resume to various job postings. The response was overwhelming, and soon, he found himself with multiple interviews lined up.

"Two weeks later, I was packing up my car," Sonny continued. "My dad asked, 'Where are you going, Son,' and I said, 'I told you, I'm moving to South Carolina.' With the support of my family, I set off with nothing but clothes and a stereo, determined to make my own way."

Reflecting on his decision, Sonny explained how he felt the need to move away from his family to truly embrace his manhood and make independent decisions.

"If I hadn't moved to South Carolina, there's a huge possibility you wouldn't be here," Sonny told Roy, his voice tinged with gratitude.

Roy's eyes widened in realization. "You're absolutely right," he replied.

Sonny continued, "If I hadn't moved, I wouldn't have reconnected with your mom, and I wouldn't have the greatest earthly gift God has given me: you, Son."

The Making of a Good Man

As they sat together, enveloped in the warmth of family and faith, Sonny and Roy reflected on the twists and turns of life's journey, grateful for the opportunities and blessings that had brought them to where they were today.

Rite of Passage and Life Targets

As they set their sights on the events of the day, Sonny had a special surprise in store for Roy: his very own BB gun. Roy's eyes sparkled with excitement as he eagerly accepted the unexpected early birthday gift from his father.

Amidst their recent father-son conversations, Sonny couldn't think of a better way to mark this rite of passage than by inviting Roy to share in some of the cherished memories he himself had experienced as a young man, playing with his cousins and their BB guns.

Knowing that their city limits weren't the ideal place for Roy to learn how to use his BB gun safely, Sonny had chosen the picturesque backdrop of Santee State Park for this momentous exchange. Setting up some old tin can targets, Sonny began to walk Roy through the basics of handling his new BB gun.

As Roy eagerly practiced his target shots, Sonny took the opportunity to share more about his own journey, particularly his move to South Carolina after college.

"I drove my Camaro 12 hours to South Carolina," Sonny recounted with a nostalgic smile. "It was the start of adulting on my own, and Central State had prepared me for that journey."

Sonny continued, sharing how he wasted no time in securing a job at a grocery store upon arrival, while also eagerly awaiting a job interview at the Greenville County Detention Center—a dream opportunity in law enforcement that he had prepared for his entire life.

"When I got the call for the job interview, I was ecstatic," Sonny recalled, the excitement evident in his voice. "And after just a week, I was hired. It was everything I had ever wanted."

Sonny's career at the detention center was marked by rapid advancement, fueled by his dedication and passion for his work. He formed close bonds with fellow officers, particularly Ronnie Drennon, with whom he shared a deep friendship that spanned over three decades.

"Ronnie Drennon and I were more than partners, we were best friends," Sonny began. "For over 30 years, we had each other's backs. We trained together, did martial arts together, and even broke bread together."

Roy's eyes widened with fascination as he listened to his father's tales of high-stakes situations and close-knit friendships.

Sonny nodded, a hint of pride in his voice. "It was an honor to work alongside such a dedicated officer. We transported some of the most high-profile criminals together, and through it all, we stood united. That kind of bond is invaluable."

As Sonny continued, he shared the highs and lows of his career at the detention center. "I was promoted three times in just three years," he explained with a sense of accomplishment in his voice. "But one day, I went up for another ranking, and I was beaten by someone more deserving."

Roy's brow furrowed with concern as he listened intently. "What did you do, Dad?" he asked.

Sonny smiled. "I congratulated the officer sincerely. I knew he deserved the position, and I believed in his work ethic. It was a tough moment, but it taught me the importance of humility and integrity in all that I do."

Sonny's thoughts drifted—a silent acknowledgment of the wisdom gained through experience. "That's the mark of a true leader, Roy," he said, his voice filled with introspection.

The Making of a Good Man

⟵―――――――――⟶

As Roy continued to practice firing his BB gun at the tin can targets, his shots consistently missed their mark, causing him to furrow his brow in frustration.

Sonny, observing his son's attempts, approached him with a reassuring smile. "Son, though I didn't get that promotion, persistence was the key," Sonny began, his voice filled with encouragement. "So, you may not have hit any of the cans yet, but I'm confident you will before today ends."

Roy nodded, determination flickering in his eyes as he readied himself to try again. "Thanks, Dad. I'll keep going," he replied, gripping the BB gun with renewed resolve.

As Roy focused on perfecting his aim, Sonny took a moment to reflect on the recent turn of events. "You know, what God has for you is for you," he remarked, his tone contemplative.

"The very next day brought unexpected news—it was a phone call from the staff at the South Carolina Criminal Justice Academy" Sonny recalled. A lady he'd trained with while working in Greenville wanted him to join her staff and train on a state-level scale."

Roy's eyes widened with excitement as he listened to his father's story unfold. "That's amazing, Dad!" he exclaimed, a proud grin spreading across his face.

Sonny's journey to becoming the youngest instructor at the academy marked a significant milestone in his career. As he immersed himself in his new role, he found himself surrounded by a supportive and influential circle of colleagues.

"The responsibility was immense," Sonny recounted, a sense of purpose infusing his words. "What I said and did from that day forward would impact the lives of every trainee across the state."

Determined to excel in his role, Sonny devoted himself to continuous improvement. "I wanted to be the best," he admitted to Roy, "so I studied harder, learned more, and applied myself to become even more marketable."

Sonny's commitment to law enforcement went beyond mere duty—it was a calling, a responsibility that weighed heavily on his shoulders. Every word he spoke, every action he took, held the potential to shape the futures of countless individuals across the state.

Realizing the magnitude of his role, Sonny knew he had to elevate his game. He thirsted for excellence, a relentless drive urging him to push himself further. To achieve this, he immersed himself in his work with unwavering dedication.

Assigned to the Detention Unit, Sonny's zeal and ambition quickly caught the attention of the academy's upper echelons. They saw in him a rare blend of passion and capability, qualities that set him apart from his peers.

Sonny's approach was meticulous. He devoured every piece of knowledge available to him, poring over lesson plans and study materials with the intensity of a scholar. His commitment was palpable, his hunger for knowledge insatiable.

But Sonny was more than just a student of the law—he was a master communicator. His classes pulsed with energy and enthusiasm, his animated delivery captivating his students' attention and leaving an indelible impact.

His passion was infectious, drawing crowds of curious onlookers who marveled at his teaching prowess. Sonny's classroom became a beacon of inspiration, a place where learning transcended mere instruction and transformed into an immersive experience.

Students from all corners of the state clamored for the opportunity to study under Sonny's tutelage. Their anticipation was matched only by their satisfaction, as each one emerged from his classes enlightened and empowered.

The accolades poured in, each glowing review a testament to Sonny's dedication and skill. Overwhelmed by the outpouring of praise, he remained humble, acknowledging God as his sole source of strength and crediting the role of his mentors and colleagues for shaping his teaching philosophy.

To Sonny, being one of the best wasn't just a goal—it was a responsibility. And as he continued to inspire and uplift those around him and his peers, he remained ever grateful to those who had helped him along the way, recognizing that his success was a testament to their collective efforts.

Roy beamed with pride at his father's achievements, feeling privileged to witness his journey firsthand. Together, they stood on the precipice of new beginnings, united by their shared commitment to success and the unwavering belief that with persistence and faith, anything was possible.

Passing the Torch

As the sun peaked, Sonny invited Roy to take a break from his target practice. Together, they sat enjoying leftovers from the day before while Sonny shared his enduring experiences with mentorship and growth that had shaped his career in law enforcement.

Sonny explained, "My journey in law enforcement wasn't just about personal growth—it was about paying it forward, passing on the invaluable lessons I had learned to the next generation of officers."

"Sam Bowser took me under his wing," Sonny began, his voice tinged with gratitude. "He was more than just a mentor; he was a guiding light in my journey."

Roy leaned in, eager to learn more about his dad's work experiences.

"Sam worked with me day in and day out. He didn't just show me the ropes of the job; he showed me how to be passionate about what I do and how teaching others only strengthens your own skills."

Nodding thoughtfully, Roy absorbed the lesson, recognizing the importance of passing on knowledge to others.

"Sam even helped me set up a 401(k)." Sonny chuckled, smiling fondly. "I didn't even know what that was at the time" explaining to Roy it was a way to make financial investments toward retirement, "but thanks to him, I'm set for the future."

As the conversation shifted, Sonny shared stories of his own journey as a mentor, particularly highlighting his bond with James Greene, a protege who had flourished under his guidance.

"James is like family now," Sonny remarked proudly. "He's on track to retire a millionaire, all because I showed him the ropes and got him involved in academy activities."

Roy listened intently, inspired by his father's commitment to helping others succeed.

But Sonny's influence extended far beyond mentoring; he was a multifaceted asset to the academy, teaching defensive tactics, building tactics, and even serving as a firearms instructor.

"Sam talked me into becoming a firearms instructor," Sonny recalled, a hint of amusement in his voice. "We went to class together, shot qualifying courses on the range together. I'll never forget the day Sam looked at my target and said it looked like it had the measles!"

Both father and son erupted into laughter, the memory of that moment a cherished reminder of the camaraderie shared with colleagues.

"Despite Sam's jest, I qualified," Sonny continued, his tone proud yet humble. "After that, I made sure I went to the range to improve my firearm proficiency. Thereafter, I was shooting an average of 220 out of 250. 180 was a qualifying score."

Roy, smiling, truly proud of his Dad's firearm skills added, "Well, Dad, maybe there's hope for me."

Sonny affirmed, "If you continue to practice—absolutely!"

On the heels of the noonday sun, father and son sat in quiet reflection, the legacy of mentorship and dedication resonating in their minds and hearts.

The Art of Instruction

With each resounding pop of Roy's BB gun, Sonny felt proud. Encouraged by his son's newfound zeal to keep practicing hitting his targets, Sonny continued sharing stories of his dedication and expertise that had defined his career in law enforcement.

"Throughout my career, I made it my mission to acquire every related certification I could," Sonny began, his voice carrying the weight of years of dedication. "I wanted to be more than just competent. I wanted to be the best."

Roy listened intently, his eyes shining with admiration for his father's accomplishments.

"I eventually rose to become the supervisor of my unit." A glimmer of humility shined in his eyes. "And together with my staff, we achieved something truly remarkable."

As he recounted the journey to earning the prestigious National Correctional Training Certification, Sonny's voice swelled with emotion.

"We were among the first in the United States to receive this honor, a testament to our dedication and expertise."

Roy nodded in understanding, beginning to grasp the magnitude of his father's impact on the field of law enforcement.

But as Sonny had shared before, he was intentional about building up those around him. He shared stories of his mentor, Paul Banner, whose passion and dedication had inspired him to become the best instructor he could be.

"Paul taught me the importance of teaching with passion and connecting with your audience," Sonny explained, his voice tinged with reverence. "And I made it my mission to carry on his legacy."

As Roy listened, Sonny delved into his teaching methods, explaining how he immersed himself in his lessons, even practicing them aloud when the classroom was empty.

"I wanted to make sure my students knew the material inside and out," Sonny emphasized, his commitment shining through his words. "Because what they learned in my class would directly impact their performance in the field."

Roy smiled, impressed by his father's dedication to his craft.

Sonny's narrative took a lighter turn as he recounted his experiences at the South Carolina Jail Association conferences, where he was a regular presenter.

"The energy I brought into the classroom was infectious," Sonny shared, a hint of mischief in his eyes. "I always made sure to make learning fun, incorporating interactive exercises and even a bit of theatrics."

Roy laughed, imagining his father's animated presence commanding the attention of every attendee.

"I was serious about delivering sound instruction, but I knew how to incorporate fun," Sonny concluded, a satisfied smile playing on his lips. "And that, my son, is the art of instruction."

Forging the Elite: Sonny's Cadre Legacy

The sun hung low in the sky, casting a golden hue over the pseudo training grounds as Roy stood, determination etched into his features. With each shot, he honed his aim, the metallic ping of his BB gun echoing through the quiet afternoon.

"Keep at it, Roy!" Sonny's voice carried across the yard, his pride evident as he watched his son persist in his practice.

After hours of relentless effort, Roy's persistence paid off. One by one, the tin cans toppled under his precise aim, a triumphant grin spreading across his face.

"Nice, Son!" Sonny's words rang out, a father's gratification evident in his tone. "You kept at it and look where it got you."

With a sense of accomplishment swelling within him, Roy glanced up at his father, their shared determination a testament to their unwavering resolve. Like father, like son—giving up was never an option for either of them.

As the sun dipped below the horizon, casting long shadows across the tree-filled landscape, Sonny and Roy began to pack up their gear, signaling the end of an incredibly memorable day. The air was cool and mixed with the scent of pine, a peaceful tranquility settling over the campgrounds.

Despite the fading light, there was a palpable sense of determination in the air, mirrored in the father and son as they prepared to head home.

As they walked side by side, the crunch of foliage underfoot, Sonny felt overwhelming joy to have had the opportunity to share these precious moments with his son. He knew that he had instilled in Roy the same unwavering commitment to excellence that had driven him throughout his own career in law enforcement.

At the pinnacle of Sonny's law enforcement career, his desire to mentor future officers burned brighter than ever. Leaning against the hood of his RV, Sonny shared with Roy the story of The Cadre Team, a legendary group of instructors at the Academy.

"Performance and practice were everything to us," Sonny explained, his voice tinged with nostalgia. "And that team—John Yarborough, Sam

Bowser, Kevin Parker, and myself—we were like a force of nature."

The Cadre Team was renowned for their discipline, their impeccable appearance, and their unwavering dedication to excellence. To Sonny, they were more than just colleagues—they were family, a brotherhood forged through shared hardship and triumph.

"Joining that team was a turning point for me," Sonny continued, his eyes alight with passion. "It pushed me to be better, to strive for greatness in everything I did."

As they loaded the last of their gear into the RV, Sonny couldn't help but feel a sense of gratitude for the journey that had brought him to this moment.

With Roy by his side, he knew that the legacy of the Cadre Team would live on, inspiring future generations of officers to strive for excellence in all they do.

With each word, Roy listened intently, captivated by his father's tales of discipline and dedication. "They were the best of the best," Sonny explained, his admiration for his former teammates evident. "And being part of that team, changed me.

"Sam Bowser, John, and Kevin—they were like superheroes," Sonny continued, a smile tugging at the corners of his lips. "Sam was built like a mountain, John was a disciplined soldier, and Kevin was a martial arts master. And me? Well, I was just trying to keep up with them."

Roy chuckled, nudging his father playfully. "Come on, Dad, I'm sure you were just as impressive as the rest of them."

Sonny's chest swelled with pride at his son's words. "Thanks, Roy. But you know, it wasn't just about being the best. It was about pushing ourselves and each other to reach new heights."

Recalling his training days with the *A train*, Sonny shared he had a drill sergeant mentality that quickly became a defining trait. He held himself to the highest standards, believing that if he asked something of his cadets, he should be able to do it—and do it better. Alongside his trusted comrade, John, Sonny led the *A train*, the elite group of cadets who had to match their pace.

Their training regimen was grueling. They started with around 10 cadets, but by the end of each run, only a select few could keep up. Sonny and John were formidable runners, their endurance unmatched. Sonny, in particular, was a machine, clocking in an impressive 26 to 36 miles per week on average.

For Sonny, a 3- to 5-mile run with the cadets was a mere warm-up. Before even meeting the group, he'd already logged several miles. It wasn't uncommon for him to meet with one of the captains at 4:30 a.m. for an early morning 3-mile run, setting the tone for the intense training session to come.

His dedication and relentless pursuit of excellence inspired those around him. While demanding, Sonny's leadership instilled a sense of discipline and determination in the cadets, pushing them to surpass their own limitations and strive for greatness. Under Sonny's guidance, the *A train* wasn't just a group—it was a force to be reckoned with, embodying the relentless spirit of its leaders.

"Dad, I'm tired just hearing about those drills," Roy interjected. "That must have been intense!"

Sonny nodded, a nostalgic glimmer in his eyes. "Oh, it was. We had to be at the top of our game, setting the example for the cadets. Believe me when I say, those early morning runs were no joke."

Roy grinned, imagining his father and John leading the pack with unwavering determination. "I bet you guys were unstoppable."

"We did our best," Sonny replied modestly, his gaze drifting off into the distance. "But it wasn't just about physical strength. It was about mental toughness, discipline, and dedication to the job."

It was evident in Sonny's voice that they were more than just a team, "We shared a brotherhood, a bond that pushed us to be our best."

As the evening wore on, the drive home carried with it stories of both Roy and Sonny's relentless pursuit of success.

As the RV hummed along the familiar route home, Sonny stole a glance at his son, Roy, expecting to find him dozing off after a long day of adventure. But to his surprise, Roy's eyes were wide open, filled with an energy that belied the late hour. Sonny couldn't help but smile at the sight of his son's excitement.

"Can't sleep, huh?" Sonny asked, his voice warm with affection.

Roy shook his head eagerly, his words tumbling out in a rush. "No way, Dad! I'm still buzzing from hitting those targets with my BB gun. It was so cool!"

Sonny chuckled, his heart swelling with pleasure at his son's enthusiasm. "I'm glad you had fun, son. You did great out there."

But Roy wasn't finished yet. "And Dad, I want to hear more about the Cadre Team. You said being on the team was the pinnacle of your career before retiring. I want to know everything!"

Sonny's smile widened at his son's eagerness to learn. "Alright, stay buckled up, Roy. I've got plenty of stories to share."

As they continued down the darkened road, Sonny regaled Roy with tales of the Cadre Team's exploits, painting vivid pictures of their discipline, dedication, and camaraderie. He shared more about the early morning runs, the rigorous training sessions, and the unforgettable moments of gratification at graduation.

"And you know, Roy," Sonny said, his voice tinged with emotion, "the greatest reward of it all was seeing my students succeed. To know that I had a hand in shaping their futures—it's a feeling like no other."

Roy listened intently, hanging onto his father's every word. He could sense that they were nearing the end of their journey, both in miles and in the stories his dad had bestowed upon him. But for Roy, the memories would last a lifetime, fueling his own dreams of one day following in his father's footsteps.

As they finally pulled into the driveway, Roy turned to his dad with a grin. "Thanks for sharing, Dad. I can't wait to hear more."

Sonny ruffled his son's hair affectionately. "Anytime, Roy. Anytime." And as they stepped out of the RV and headed inside, father and son carried with them the legacy of the Cadre Team and a bond that would endure long after the stars had faded from the sky.

Carrying the Torch: A Lifetime of Service and Sacrifice

As they settled home, Sonny thought it fitting to end the evening summing up his final days with law enforcement. Roy leaned in eagerly, ready to absorb every detail of his father's illustrious career. Sonny's eyes sparkled with a mixture of joy and nostalgia as he began to recount the countless lives he had touched throughout his 29 years of service.

"I taught law enforcement officers for 29 years," he began, his voice carrying the weight of decades of experience. "I had 10 to 12 detention officers' classes and 15 classes a year of street officers, each with 70 students. That adds up to over 50 thousand officers whose lives I've impacted."

Roy's eyes widened in awe at the sheer magnitude of his father's influence. "Wow, that's incredible, Dad."

Sonny nodded, a small smile playing on his lips. "Wherever I go in South Carolina, someone knows me," he continued. "They stop me and share stories of how something I taught them saved their lives."

Despite the routine nature of his daily schedule, Sonny approached each day with renewed enthusiasm. "I wanted to make sure my students learned the tactics they needed to know to keep them safe. I wanted them to be the best they could be in law enforcement."

Roy listened intently, his father's words resonating deep within him. "But not everyone took training as seriously as they should have," Sonny continued, his tone growing somber. "Some officers only wanted to get by, to take shortcuts. But I knew that the way you train is the way you'll perform."

Sonny's expression darkened as he recounted the officers who had paid the ultimate price due to their lack of commitment to training. "It's heartbreaking to see officers get hurt or killed on the job because they didn't take training seriously," he said, his voice heavy with regret. "I used to warn my cadets that they were headed down a dangerous path if they didn't work to improve their skills."

Listening to his father's words, Roy felt a lump form in his throat. He could sense the weight of responsibility in his dad's tone, a burden borne from years of experience and dedication to his profession.

Sonny's gaze drifted into the distance as he remembered those he had lost in the line of duty. "I did everything I could to instill in my students the importance of commitment, excellence, and protecting the community," he said quietly, his voice tinged with sorrow.

As the evening wore on, Roy sat in quiet reflection, his father's stories swirling in his mind. He couldn't shake the sense of admiration and respect he felt for his father Sonny, a man who had dedicated his life to serving others and ensuring the safety of his community.

Finally, as they bid each other goodnight, Roy felt a newfound appreciation for his father's legacy. Sonny's lessons, both spoken and unspoken, would continue to shape Roy's own path forward. And as he drifted off to sleep, Roy carried with him the knowledge that his father's commitment to excellence would live on, not just in the lives he had touched, but in the heart of his son.

This father-son journey of shared stories began with Roy's question to his Mom, "Mama, how can I become a good man?" However, he was immensely grateful his dad was there to not only tell him but to also model the characteristics of a good man.

Roy knew he had a long way to go before becoming a man, but he was confident that with the ever-present support of his Granny, Mom, Dad, and his extended family, he was a boy in training who, by God's grace, would grow to become a good man. As he drifted into dreams, Roy carried with him a sense of purpose and determination, knowing that he walked in the footsteps of a great man: his Dad.

www.ingramcontent.com/pod-product-compliance
Lightning Source LLC
Chambersburg PA
CBHW072043160426
43197CB00014B/2614